# MznLnx

*Missing Links Exam Preps*

Exam Prep for

# Finite Mathematics: For Business, Economics, Life Sciences, and Social Sciences

Barnett, Ziegler, & Byleen, 11th Edition

The MznLnx Exam Prep is your link from the texbook and lecture to your exams.
The MznLnx Exam Preps are unauthorized and comprehensive reviews of your textbooks.

All material provided by MznLnx and Rico Publications (c) 2010
Textbook publishers and textbook authors do not particpate in or contribute to these reviews.

# MznLnx

## Rico Publications

*Exam Prep for Finite Mathematics: For Business, Economics, Life Sciences, and Social Sciences*
11th Edition
Barnett, Ziegler, & Byleen

*Publisher:* Raymond Houge
*Assistant Editor:* Michael Rouger
*Text and Cover Designer:* Lisa Buckner
*Marketing Manager:* Sara Swagger
*Project Manager, Editorial Production:* Jerry Emerson
*Art Director:* Vernon Lowerui

*Product Manager:* Dave Mason
*Editorial Assitant:* Rachel Guzmanji
*Pedagogy:* Debra Long
*Cover Image:* Jim Reed/Getty Images
*Text and Cover Printer:* City Printing, Inc.
*Compositor:* Media Mix, Inc.

(c) 2010 Rico Publications
ALL RIGHTS RESERVED. No part of this work covered by the copyright may be reproduced or used in any form or by an means--graphic, electronic, or mechanical, including photocopying, recording, taping, Web distribution, information storage, and retrieval systems, or in any other manner--without the written permission of the publisher.

Printed in the United States
ISBN:

For more information about our products, contact us at:
Dave.Mason@RicoPublications.com

For permission to use material from this text or product, submit a request online to:
Dave.Mason@RicoPublications.com

# Contents

**CHAPTER 1**
*Linear Equations and Graphs* … 1

**CHAPTER 2**
*Functions and Graphs* … 17

**CHAPTER 3**
*Mathematics of Finance* … 35

**CHAPTER 4**
*Systems of Linear Equations; Matrices* … 42

**CHAPTER 5**
*Linear Inequalities and Linear Programming* … 55

**CHAPTER 6**
*Linear Programming: Simplex Method* … 63

**CHAPTER 7**
*Logic, Sets, and Counting* … 73

**CHAPTER 8**
*Probability* … 84

**CHAPTER 9**
*Markov Chains* … 96

**CHAPTER 10**
*Games and Decisions* … 103

**CHAPTER 11**
*Data Description and Probability Distributions* … 110

**ANSWER KEY** … 125

# TO THE STUDENT

## COMPREHENSIVE

The *MznLnx* Exam Prep series is designed to help you pass your exams. Editors at MznLnx review your textbooks and then prepare these practice exams to help you master the textbook material. Unlike study guides, workbooks, and practice tests provided by the texbook publisher and textbook authors, *MznLnx* gives you **all** of the material in each chapter in exam form, not just samples, so you can be sure to nail your exam.

## MECHANICAL

The MznLnx Exam Prep series creates exams that will help you learn the subject matter as well as test you on your understanding. Each question is designed to help you master the concept. Just working through the exams, you gain an understanding of the subject--its a simple mechanical process that produces success.

## INTEGRATED STUDY GUIDE AND REVIEW

MznLnx is not just a set of exams designed to test you, its also a comprehensive review of the subject content. Each exam question is also a review of the concept, making sure that you will get the answer correct without having to go to other sources of material. You learn as you go! Its the easiest way to pass an exam.

## HUMOR

Studying can be tedious and dry. MznLnx's instructional design includes moderate humor within the exam questions on occassion, to break the tedium and revitalize the brain

## Chapter 1. Linear Equations and Graphs

1. A _____ is a structured activity, usually undertaken for enjoyment and sometimes also used as an educational tool. _____s are distinct from work, which is usually carried out for remuneration, and from art, which is more concerned with the expression of ideas. However, the distinction is not clear-cut, and many _____s are also considered to be work (such as professional players of spectator sports/_____s) or art (such as jigsaw puzzles or _____s involving an artistic layout such as Mah-jongg solitaire.)
   a. 2-3 heap
   b. 120-cell
   c. Game
   d. 1-center problem

2. In mathematics, _____ is a technique for optimization of a linear objective function, subject to linear equality and linear inequality constraints. Informally, _____ determines the way to achieve the best outcome in a given mathematical model given some list of requirements represented as linear equations.

   More formally, given a polytope, and a real-valued affine function

   $$f(x_1, x_2, \ldots, x_n) = c_1 x_1 + c_2 x_2 + \cdots + c_n x_n + d$$

   defined on this polytope, a _____ method will find a point in the polytope where this function has the smallest value.

   a. Descent direction
   b. Lin-Kernighan
   c. Linear programming
   d. Linear programming relaxation

3. The function $\log_b(x)$ depends on both b and x, but the term _____ (or logarithmic function) in standard usage refers to a function of the form $\log_b(x)$ in which the base b is fixed and so the only argument is x. Thus there is one _____ for each value of the base b (which must be positive and must differ from 1.) Viewed in this way, the base-b _____ is the inverse function of the exponential function $b^x$.
   a. 2-3 heap
   b. 1-center problem
   c. Logarithm function
   d. 120-cell

4. A _____ is a software program that facilitates symbolic mathematics. The core functionality of a CAS is manipulation of mathematical expressions in symbolic form.

The symbolic manipulations supported typically include

- simplification to the smallest possible expression or some standard form, including automatic simplification with assumptions and simplification with constraints
- substitution of symbolic, functors or numeric values for expressions
- change of form of expressions: expanding products and powers, partial and full factorization, rewriting as partial fractions, constraint satisfaction, rewriting trigonometric functions as exponentials, etc.
- partial and total differentiation
- symbolic constrained and unconstrained global optimization
- solution of linear and some non-linear equations over various domains
- solution of some differential and difference equations
- taking some limits
- some indefinite and definite integration, including multidimensional integrals
- integral transforms
- arbitrary-precision numeric operations
- Series operations such as expansion, summation and products
- matrix operations including products, inverses, etc.
- display of mathematical expressions in two-dimensional mathematical form, often using typesetting systems similar to TeX
- add-ons for use in applied mathematics such as physics packages for physical computation
- plotting graphs and parametric plots of functions in two and three dimensions, and animating them
- APIs for linking it on an external program such as a database, or using in a programming language to use the _____
- drawing charts and diagrams
- string manipulation such as matching and searching
- statistical computation
- Theorem proving and verification
- graphic production and editing such as CGI and signal processing as image processing
- sound synthesis

Many also include a programming language, allowing users to implement their own algorithms.

Some _____s focus on a specific area of application; these are typically developed in academia and are free.

a. Computer algebra system
b. 1-center problem
c. 2-3 heap
d. 120-cell

5. In mathematics and computer science, _____ (also base-16, hexa or base, of 16. It uses sixteen distinct symbols, most often the symbols 0-9 to represent values zero to nine, and A, B, C, D, E, F (or a through f) to represent values ten to fifteen.

Its primary use is as a human friendly representation of binary coded values, so it is often used in digital electronics and computer engineering.

   a. Factoradic
   b. Radix
   c. Hexadecimal
   d. Tetradecimal


6. The mathematical concept of a _____ expresses the intuitive idea of deterministic dependence between two quantities, one of which is viewed as primary and the other as secondary. A _____ then is a way to associate a unique output for each input of a specified type, for example, a real number or an element of a given set.
   a. Grill
   b. Function
   c. Coherent
   d. Going up


7. In game theory, a player's _____ in a game is a complete plan of action for whatever situation might arise; this fully determines the player's behaviour. A player's _____ will determine the action the player will take at any stage of the game, for every possible history of play up to that stage.

A _____ profile is a set of strategies for each player which fully specifies all actions in a game.

   a. Strategy
   b. Sir Philip Sidney game
   c. Matching pennies
   d. Correlated equilibrium


8. In the study of metric spaces in mathematics, there are various notions of two metrics on the same underlying space being 'the same', or _____.

In the following, M will denote a non-empty set and $d_1$ and $d_2$ will denote two metrics on M.

The two metrics $d_1$ and $d_2$ are said to be topologically _____ if they generate the same topology on M.

a. A posteriori
b. A chemical equation
c. A Mathematical Theory of Communication
d. Equivalent

9. A _____ is an algebraic equation in which each term is either a constant or the product of a constant and a single variable. _____s can have one, two, three or more variables.

_____s occur with great regularity in applied mathematics.

a. Linear equation
b. Difference of two squares
c. Quartic equation
d. Quadratic equation

10. In mathematics a _____ is an inequality which involves a linear function.

When operating in terms of real numbers, linear inequalities are the ones written in the forms

$$f(x) < b \text{ or } f(x) \leq b,$$

where f(x) is a linear functional in real numbers and b is a constant real number. Alternatively, these may be viewed as

$$g(x) < 0 \text{ or } g(x) \leq 0,$$

where g(x) is an affine function.

a. Split-complex number
b. Generalized singular value decomposition
c. Levi-Civita symbol
d. Linear inequality

11. In mathematics, _____ and undefined are used to explain whether or not expressions have meaningful, sensible, and unambiguous values. Not all branches of mathematics come to the same conclusion.

The following expressions are undefined in all contexts, but remarks in the analysis section may apply.

a. Defined
b. Toy model
c. LHS
d. Plugging in



12. In mathematics, an _____ is a statement about the relative size or order of two objects, or about whether they are the same or not

- The notation a < b means that a is less than b.
- The notation a > b means that a is greater than b.
- The notation a ≠ b means that a is not equal to b, but does not say that one is bigger than the other or even that they can be compared in size.

In all these cases, a is not equal to b, hence, '_____'.

These relations are known as strict _____

- The notation a ≤ b means that a is less than or equal to b;
- The notation a ≥ b means that a is greater than or equal to b;

An additional use of the notation is to show that one quantity is much greater than another, normally by several orders of magnitude.

- The notation a << b means that a is much less than b.
- The notation a >> b means that a is much greater than b.

If the sense of the _____ is the same for all values of the variables for which its members are defined, then the _____ is called an 'absolute' or 'unconditional' _____. If the sense of an _____ holds only for certain values of the variables involved, but is reversed or destroyed for other values of the variables, it is called a conditional _____.

An _____ may appear unsolvable because it only states whether a number is larger or smaller than another number; but it is possible to apply the same operations for equalities to inequalities. For example, to find x for the _____ 10x > 23 one would divide 23 by 10.

a. A Mathematical Theory of Communication
b. A chemical equation
c. A posteriori
d. Inequality

13. In mathematics and in the sciences, a _____ (plural: _____e, formulæ or _____s) is a concise way of expressing information symbolically (as in a mathematical or chemical _____), or a general relationship between quantities. One of many famous _____e is Albert Einstein's E = mc² (see special relativity

In mathematics, a _____ is a key to solve an equation with variables. For example, the problem of determining the volume of a sphere is one that requires a significant amount of integral calculus to solve.

   a. 2-3 heap
   b. Formula
   c. 120-cell
   d. 1-center problem


14. In mathematics, a _____ is a set of real numbers with the property that any number that lies between two numbers in the set is also included in the set. For example, the set of all numbers x satisfying $0 \leq x \leq 1$ is an _____ which contains 0 and 1, as well as all numbers between them. Other examples of _____s are the set of all real numbers $\mathbb{R}$, the set of all positive real numbers, and the empty set.
   a. Annihilator
   b. Order
   c. Interval
   d. Ideal


15. _____ is the notation in which permitted values for a variable are expressed as ranging over a certain interval; "5 < x < 9" is an example of the application of _____.
   a. Interval notation
   b. Infinity
   c. A Mathematical Theory of Communication
   d. Implicit differentiation


16. In a graph theory, the _____ L

One of the earliest and most important theorems about _____s is due to Hassler Whitney, who proved that with one exceptional case the structure of G can be recovered completely from its _____.

   a. Vertex-transitive graph
   b. Line graph
   c. Sparse graph
   d. Bivariegated graph

## Chapter 1. Linear Equations and Graphs

17. In mathematics, especially in the area of abstract algebra known as combinatorial group theory, the _____ for a recursively presented group G is the algorithmic problem of deciding whether two words represent the same element. Although it is common to speak of the _____ for the group G strictly speaking it is a presentation of the group that does or does not have solvable _____. Given two finite presentations P and Q of a group G, P has solvable _____ if and only if Q does.
   a. Word problem
   b. Prime ideal theorem
   c. Computational mathematics
   d. Torsion

18. In economics, business, retail, and accounting, a _____ is the value of money that has been used up to produce something, and hence is not available for use anymore. In business, the _____ may be one of acquisition, in which case the amount of money expended to acquire it is counted as _____. In this case, money is the input that is gone in order to acquire the thing.
   a. 1-center problem
   b. 2-3 heap
   c. 120-cell
   d. Cost

19. The x-axis is the horizontal axis of a two- dimensional plot in the _____, that is typically pointed to the right. Also known as a right-handed coordinate system.
   a. 2-3 heap
   b. Cartesian coordinate system
   c. 1-center problem
   d. 120-cell

20. In mathematics, the _____ is an approach to finding a particular solution to certain inhomogeneous ordinary differential equations and recurrence relations. It is closely related to the annihilator method, but instead of using a particular kind of differential operator in order to find the best possible form of the particular solution, a 'guess' is made as to the appropriate form, which is then tested by differentiating the resulting equation. In this sense, the _____ is less formal but more intuitive than the annihilator method.
   a. Differential algebraic equations
   b. Method of undetermined coefficients
   c. Phase line
   d. Linear differential equation

# Chapter 1. Linear Equations and Graphs

21. _____ is the study of geometry using the principles of algebra. That the algebra of the real numbers can be employed to yield results about the linear continuum of geometry relies on the Cantor-Dedekind axiom. Usually the Cartesian coordinate system is applied to manipulate equations for planes, straight lines, and squares, often in two and sometimes in three dimensions of measurement.
    a. Axis-aligned object
    b. Analytic geometry
    c. Angular eccentricity
    d. Ambient space

22. In quantum field theory and statistical mechanics in the thermodynamic limit, a system with a global symmetry can have more than one phase. For parameters where the symmetry is spontaneously broken, the system is said to be _____. When the global symmetry is unbroken the system is disordered.
    a. Ordered
    b. Ursell function
    c. Einstein relation
    d. Isoenthalpic-isobaric ensemble

23. In mathematics, an _____ is a collection of objects having two coordinates (or entries or projections), such that one can always uniquely determine the object, which is the first coordinate (or first entry or left projection) of the pair as well as the second coordinate (or second entry or right projection.) If the first coordinate is a and the second is b, the usual notation for an _____ is (a, b.) The pair is 'ordered' in that (a, b) differs from (b, a) unless a = b.
    a. A posteriori
    b. A Mathematical Theory of Communication
    c. A chemical equation
    d. Ordered pair

24. In mathematics, the _____ of a Euclidean space is a special point, usually denoted by the letter O, used as a fixed point of reference for the geometry of the surrounding space. In a Cartesian coordinate system, the _____ is the point where the axes of the system intersect. In Euclidean geometry, the _____ may be chosen freely as any convenient point of reference.
    a. OMAC
    b. Interval
    c. Autonomous system
    d. Origin

25. A _____ consists of one quarter of the coordinate plane.

*Chapter 1. Linear Equations and Graphs* 9

a. 2-3 heap
b. Quadrant
c. 120-cell
d. 1-center problem

26. _____ is a part of mathematics concerned with questions of size, shape, and relative position of figures and with properties of space. _____ is one of the oldest sciences. Initially a body of practical knowledge concerning lengths, areas, and volumes, in the third century BC _____ was put into an axiomatic form by Euclid, whose treatment--Euclidean _____--set a standard for many centuries to follow.
   a. 120-cell
   b. Geometry
   c. 2-3 heap
   d. 1-center problem

27. In mathematics, the _____s may be described informally in several different ways. The _____s include both rational numbers, such as 42 and −23/129, and irrational numbers, such as pi and the square root of two; or, a _____ can be given by an infinite decimal representation, such as 2.4871773339...., where the digits continue in some way; or, the _____s may be thought of as points on an infinitely long number line.

These descriptions of the _____s, while intuitively accessible, are not sufficiently rigorous for the purposes of pure mathematics.

   a. Real number
   b. Pre-algebra
   c. Tally marks
   d. Minkowski distance

28. In mathematics, a _____ is a statement that can be proved on the basis of explicitly stated or previously agreed assumptions.
   a. Theorem
   b. Disjunction introduction
   c. Logical value
   d. Boolean function

29. _____, also sometimes known as standard form or as exponential notation, is a way of writing numbers that accommodates values too large or small to be conveniently written in standard decimal notation. _____ has a number of useful properties and is often favored by scientists, mathematicians and engineers, who work with such numbers.

In _____, numbers are written in the form:

$$a \times 10^b$$

a. Scientific notation
b. Leading zero
c. 1-center problem
d. Radix point

30. A _____ typically refers to a class of handheld calculators that are capable of plotting graphs, solving simultaneous equations, and performing numerous other tasks with variables. Most popular _____s are also programmable, allowing the user to create customized programs, typically for scientific/engineering and education applications. Due to their large displays intended for graphing, they can also accommodate several lines of text and calculations at a time.

   a. Bump mapping
   b. Genus
   c. Support vector machines
   d. Graphing calculator

31. In linear algebra, the _____ of an n-by-n square matrix A is defined to be the sum of the elements on the main diagonal of A. wikimedia.org/math/8/2/b/82be32fa00bd97ebbc066aec3dfe72da.png">

where $a_{ij}$ represents the entry on the ith row and jth column of A. Equivalently, the _____ of a matrix is the sum of its eigenvalues, making it an invariant with respect to a change of basis.

   a. Blinding
   b. TRACE
   c. Lattice
   d. Constructivism

32. A _____ is a device for performing mathematical calculations, distinguished from a computer by having a limited problem solving ability and an interface optimized for interactive calculation rather than programming. _____s can be hardware or software, and mechanical or electronic, and are often built into devices such as PDAs or mobile phones.

Modern electronic _____s are generally small, digital, and usually inexpensive.

*Chapter 1. Linear Equations and Graphs* 11

    a. 1-center problem
    b. 120-cell
    c. 2-3 heap
    d. Calculator

33. _____ is used to describe the steepness, incline, gradient, or grade of a straight line. A higher _____ value indicates a steeper incline. The _____ is defined as the ratio of the 'rise' divided by the 'run' between two points on a line, or in other words, the ratio of the altitude change to the horizontal distance between any two points on the line.
    a. Point plotting
    b. Cognitively Guided Instruction
    c. Number line
    d. Slope

34. _____ is a form where m is the slope of the line and b is the y-intercept, which is the y-coordinate of the point where the line crosses the y axis. This can be seen by letting x = 0, which immediately gives y = b.
    a. Commutative law
    b. Separable extension
    c. Dynamical system
    d. Slope-intercept form

35. The _____ expresses the fact that the difference in the y coordinate between two points on a line that is, y − y1 is proportional to the difference in the x coordinate that is, x − x1. The proportionality constant is m (the slope of the line.
    a. Rubin Causal Model
    b. Cobb-Douglas
    c. Square function
    d. Point-slope form

36. In mathematics, hyperbolic n-space, denoted $H^n$, is the maximally symmetric, simply connected, n-dimensional Riemannian manifold with constant sectional curvature −1. _____ is the principal example of a space exhibiting hyperbolic geometry. It can be thought of as the negative-curvature analogue of the n-sphere.
    a. Hyperbolic geometry
    b. Margulis lemma
    c. Horocycle
    d. Hyperbolic space

37. In mathematics, the point $\tilde{x} \in \mathbb{R}^n$ is an _____ for the differential equation

$$\frac{d\mathbf{x}}{dt} = \mathbf{f}(t, \mathbf{x})$$

if $\mathbf{f}(t, \tilde{\mathbf{x}}) = 0$ for all $t$.

Similarly, the point $\tilde{\mathbf{x}} \in \mathbb{R}^n$ is an _____ for the difference equation

$$\mathbf{x}_{k+1} = \mathbf{f}(k, \mathbf{x}_k)$$

if $\mathbf{f}(k, \tilde{\mathbf{x}}) = \tilde{\mathbf{x}}$ for $k = 0, 1, 2, \ldots$.

Equilibria can be classified by looking at the signs of the eigenvalues of the linearization of the equations about the equilibria.

a. Algorithm design
b. Uniform algebra
c. Unitary transformation
d. Equilibrium point


38. In statistics, _____ is a form of regression analysis in which the relationship between one or more independent variables and another variable, called dependent variable, is modeled by a least squares function, called _____ equation. This function is a linear combination of one or more model parameters, called regression coefficients. A _____ equation with one independent variable represents a straight line.
    a. Percentile rank
    b. Random variables
    c. Kurtosis
    d. Linear regression


39. A _____ is an abstract model that uses mathematical language to describe the behavior of a system. Eykhoff defined a _____ as 'a representation of the essential aspects of an existing system which presents knowledge of that system in usable form'.
    a. Mathematical model
    b. Rata Die
    c. Metaheuristic
    d. Total least squares

40. The _____ fallacy is an informal fallacy. It ascribes cause where none exists. The flaw is failing to account for natural fluctuations.
   a. Degrees of freedom
   b. Depth
   c. Differential
   d. Regression


41. In mathematics, an _____, or central tendency of a data set refers to a measure of the 'middle' or 'expected' value of the data set. There are many different descriptive statistics that can be chosen as a measurement of the central tendency of the data items.

An _____ is a single value that is meant to typify a list of values.

   a. Average
   b. A chemical equation
   c. A posteriori
   d. A Mathematical Theory of Communication


42. In physiology and medicine, the _____ BSA is the measured or calculated surface of a human body. For many clinical purposes BSA is a better indicator of metabolic mass than body weight because it is less affected by abnormal adipose mass. Estimation of BSA is simpler than many measures of volume.
   a. Cobb-Douglas
   b. Metaheuristic
   c. Body surface area
   d. Non-linear least squares


43. _____ is a quantity expressing the two-dimensional size of a defined part of a surface, typically a region bounded by a closed curve. The term surface _____ refers to the total _____ of the exposed surface of a 3-dimensional solid, such as the sum of the _____s of the exposed sides of a polyhedron. _____ is an important invariant in the differential geometry of surfaces.
   a. A Mathematical Theory of Communication
   b. Area
   c. A posteriori
   d. A chemical equation


44. In mathematics, the idea of _____ has come to stand for a very general idea, extending the intuitive idea of 'gluing' in topology. Since the topologists' glue is actually the use of equivalence relations on topological spaces, the theory starts with some ideas on identification.

A sophisticated theory resulted.

   a. Deviance
   b. Dominance
   c. Descent
   d. Block size

45. In mathematics, specifically in topology, a _____ is a two-dimensional manifold. The most familiar examples are those that arise as the boundaries of solid objects in ordinary three-dimensional Euclidean space, EÂ³. On the other hand, there are also more exotic _____s, that are so 'contorted' that they cannot be embedded in three-dimensional space at all.
   a. Standard torus
   b. Homoeoid
   c. Surface
   d. Cross-cap

46. _____ is how much exposed area an object has. It is expressed in square units. If an object has flat faces, its _____ can be calculated by adding together the areas of its faces.
   a. Relative dimension
   b. Compactness measure of a shape
   c. Surface area
   d. Reflection group

47. In mathematics, the concept of a _____ tries to capture the intuitive idea of a geometrical one-dimensional and continuous object. A simple example is the circle. In everyday use of the term '_____', a straight line is not curved, but in mathematical parlance _____s include straight lines and line segments.
   a. Curve
   b. Quadrifolium
   c. Kappa curve
   d. Negative pedal curve

48. _____ is finding a curve which has the best fit to a series of data points and possibly other constraints. This section is an introduction to both interpolation and regression analysis. Both are sometimes used for extrapolation.

## Chapter 1. Linear Equations and Graphs

a. Multiphysics
b. Spectral methods
c. Numerical stability
d. Curve fitting

49. In statistics, _____ is a collective name for techniques for the modeling and analysis of numerical data consisting of values of a dependent variable and of one or more independent variables. The dependent variable in the regression equation is modeled as a function of the independent variables, corresponding parameters, and an error term. The error term is treated as a random variable.

a. 120-cell
b. Regression analysis
c. 2-3 heap
d. 1-center problem

50. A _____ is a type of display using Cartesian coordinates to display values for two variables for a set of data. The data is displayed as a collection of points, each having the value of one variable determining the position on the horizontal axis and the value of the other variable determining the position on the vertical axis. A _____ is also called a scatter chart, scatter diagram and scatter graph.

a. Scatter plot
b. 120-cell
c. 1-center problem
d. 2-3 heap

51. A _____ is is a graphical technique for presenting a data set drawn by hand or produced by a mechanical or electronic plotter. It is a graph depicting the relationship between two or more variables used, for instance, in visualising scientific data.

_____s play an important role in statistics and data analysis.

a. Lattice
b. Plot
c. Dini
d. C-35

52. _____ is a method of constructing new data points from a discrete set of known data points.

a. Archimedes' use of infinitesimals
b. Interpolation
c. Integration by substitution
d. Uniform convergence

53. _____ is the measurement of vertical distance, but has two meanings in common use. It can either indicate how 'tall' something is, or how 'high up' it is. For example one could say 'That is a tall building', or 'That airplane is high up in the sky'.
    a. 120-cell
    b. 2-3 heap
    c. 1-center problem
    d. Height

54. In set theory, a _____ is a partially ordered set such that for each t ∈ T, the set {s ∈ T : s < t} is well-ordered by the relation <. For each t ∈ T, the order type of {s ∈ T : s < t} is called the height of t. The height of T itself is the least ordinal greater than the height of each element of T.
    a. Transitive reduction
    b. Definable numbers
    c. Set-theoretic topology
    d. Tree

## Chapter 2. Functions and Graphs

1. The mathematical concept of a _____ expresses the intuitive idea of deterministic dependence between two quantities, one of which is viewed as primary and the other as secondary. A _____ then is a way to associate a unique output for each input of a specified type, for example, a real number or an element of a given set.
   a. Going up
   b. Grill
   c. Function
   d. Coherent

2. In mathematics, _____ and undefined are used to explain whether or not expressions have meaningful, sensible, and unambiguous values. Not all branches of mathematics come to the same conclusion.

   The following expressions are undefined in all contexts, but remarks in the analysis section may apply.

   a. Plugging in
   b. LHS
   c. Toy model
   d. Defined

3. _____ and independent variables refer to values that change in relationship to each other. The _____ are those that are observed to change in response to the independent variables. The independent variables are those that are deliberately manipulated to invoke a change in the _____.
   a. Yates analysis
   b. Round robin test
   c. Dependent variables
   d. Steiner system

4. Dependent variables and _____ refer to values that change in relationship to each other. The dependent variables are those that are observed to change in response to the _____. The _____ are those that are deliberately manipulated to invoke a change in the dependent variables.
   a. One-factor-at-a-time method
   b. Experimental design diagram
   c. Independent variables
   d. Operational confound

5. In vascular plants, the _____ is the organ of a plant body that typically lies below the surface of the soil. This is not always the case, however, since a _____ can also be aerial (that is, growing above the ground) or aerating (that is, growing up above the ground or especially above water.) Furthermore, a stem normally occurring below ground is not exceptional either

a. 120-cell
b. 1-center problem
c. Root
d. 2-3 heap

6. In mathematics, a _____ of a number x is a number r such that $r^2$ = x, or, in other words, a number r whose square is x. Every non-negative real number x has a unique non-negative _____, called the principal _____, which is denoted with a radical symbol as $\sqrt{x}$, or, using exponent notation, as $x^{1/2}$. For example, the principal _____ of 9 is 3, denoted $\sqrt{9}$ = 3, because $3^2$ = 3 × 3 = 9.
   a. Hyperbolic functions
   b. Double exponential
   c. Multiplicative inverse
   d. Square root

7. In mathematics, a _____ is a function whose values do not vary and thus are constant. For example, if we have the function f→ B is a _____ if f
   a. Point reflection
   b. Squeeze mapping
   c. Linear operator
   d. Constant function

8. In mathematics, especially in the area of abstract algebra known as ring theory, a _____ is a ring with 0 ≠ 1 such that ab = 0 implies that either a = 0 or b = 0. That is, it is a nontrivial ring without left or right zero divisors. A commutative _____ is called an integral _____.
   a. Simple ring
   b. Modular representation theory
   c. Domain
   d. Left primitive ring

9. In mathematics, a _____ is the end result of a division problem. It can also be expressed as the number of times the divisor divides into the dividend.
   a. Marginal cost
   b. Limiting
   c. Notation
   d. Quotient

## Chapter 2. Functions and Graphs

10. In economics, business, retail, and accounting, a _____ is the value of money that has been used up to produce something, and hence is not available for use anymore. In business, the _____ may be one of acquisition, in which case the amount of money expended to acquire it is counted as _____. In this case, money is the input that is gone in order to acquire the thing.
    a. 1-center problem
    b. Cost
    c. 2-3 heap
    d. 120-cell

11. In economics, the cross elasticity of demand and _____ measures the responsiveness of the quantity demanded of a good to a change in the price of another good.

It is measured as the percentage change in quantity demanded for the first good that occurs in response to a percentage change in price of the second good. For example, if, in response to a 10% increase in the price of fuel, the quantity of new cars that are fuel inefficient demanded decreased by 20%, the cross elasticity of demand would be -20%/10% = -2.

   a. Supply and demand
   b. 1-center problem
   c. Marginal rate of substitution
   d. Cross price elasticity of demand

12. A _____ is an abstract model that uses mathematical language to describe the behavior of a system. Eykhoff defined a _____ as 'a representation of the essential aspects of an existing system which presents knowledge of that system in usable form'.
    a. Total least squares
    b. Rata Die
    c. Metaheuristic
    d. Mathematical model

13. _____ expresses an annual rate of interest taking into account the effect of compounding, usually for deposit or investment products. It is analogous to the Annual percentage rate, which is used for loans. In some jurisdictions, the use and definition of _____ may be regulated by a government agency, in which case it would generally be capitalized.
    a. A chemical equation
    b. A posteriori
    c. A Mathematical Theory of Communication
    d. Annual percentage yield

14. In computational complexity theory, the complexity class _____ is the union of the classes in the exponential hierarchy.

$$\begin{aligned}\text{ELEMENTARY} &= \text{EXP} \cup 2\text{EXP} \cup 3\text{EXP} \cup \cdots \\ &= \text{DTIME}(2^n) \cup \text{DTIME}(2^{2^n}) \cup \text{DTIME}(2^{2^{2^n}}) \cup \cdots\end{aligned}$$

The name was coined by Laszlo Kalmar, in the context of recursive functions and undecidability; most problems in it are far from _____. Some natural recursive problems lie outside _____, and are thus NONELEMENTARY.

   a. A chemical equation
   b. A posteriori
   c. A Mathematical Theory of Communication
   d. Elementary


15. In mathematics, an _____ is a function built from a finite number of exponentials, logarithms, constants, one variable, and roots of equations through composition and combinations using the four elementary operations (+ - × ÷.) The trigonometric functions and their inverses are assumed to be included in the _____s by using complex variables and the relations between the trigonometric functions and the exponential and logarithm functions.

_____s are considered a subset of special functions.

   a. A chemical equation
   b. A Mathematical Theory of Communication
   c. A posteriori
   d. Elementary function


16. In mathematics, a _____ is a way of expressing a number as a fraction of 100. It is often denoted using the percent sign, '%'. For example, 45% is equal to 45 / 100, or 0.45.
   a. Subtrahend
   b. Lowest common denominator
   c. Least common multiple
   d. Percentage


17. In mathematics, the _____ of a real number is its numerical value without regard to its sign. So, for example, 3 is the _____ of both 3 and −3.

The _____ of a number a is denoted by $|a|$.

## Chapter 2. Functions and Graphs

Generalizations of the _____ for real numbers occur in a wide variety of mathematical settings.

a. A chemical equation
b. A Mathematical Theory of Communication
c. Area hyperbolic functions
d. Absolute value

18. A _____ of a number is a number a such that $a^3 = x$.
a. Golden function
b. Hyperbolic functions
c. Square root
d. Cube root

19. In mathematics, the term _____ has several different important meanings:

- An _____ is an equality that remains true regardless of the values of any variables that appear within it, to distinguish it from an equality which is true under more particular conditions. For this, the 'triple bar' symbol ≡ is sometimes used.
- In algebra, an _____ or _____ element of a set S with a binary operation Â· is an element e that, when combined with any element x of S, produces that same x. That is, eÂ·x = xÂ·e = x for all x in S.
  - The _____ function from a set S to itself, often denoted id or id$_S$, s the function such that i = x for all x in S. This function serves as the _____ element in the set of all functions from S to itself with respect to function composition.
  - In linear algebra, the _____ matrix of size n is the n-by-n square matrix with ones on the main diagonal and zeros elsewhere. This matrix serves as the _____ with respect to matrix multiplication.

A common example of the first meaning is the trigonometric _____

$$\sin^2 \theta + \cos^2 \theta = 1$$

which is true for all real values of θ, as opposed to

$$\cos \theta = 1,$$

which is true only for some values of θ, not all. For example, the latter equation is true when $\theta = 0$, false when $\theta = 2$

## Chapter 2. Functions and Graphs

The concepts of 'additive _____' and 'multiplicative _____' are central to the Peano axioms. The number 0 is the 'additive _____' for integers, real numbers, and complex numbers. For the real numbers, for all $a \in \mathbb{R}$,

$$0 + a = a,$$

$$a + 0 = a, \text{ and}$$

$$0 + 0 = 0.$$

Similarly, The number 1 is the 'multiplicative _____' for integers, real numbers, and complex numbers.

a. Identity
b. ARIA
c. Action
d. Intersection


20. An _____ is a function that does not have any effect: it always returns the same value that was used as its argument.
    a. Algebra
    b. Inverse function
    c. Identity function
    d. Angle bisector


21. In descriptive statistics, the _____ is the length of the smallest interval which contains all the data. It is calculated by subtracting the smallest observations from the greatest and provides an indication of statistical dispersion.

It is measured in the same units as the data.

a. Kernel
b. Range
c. Class
d. Bandwidth


22. In mathematics, a _____ is a square root of a function with respect to the operation of function composition. In other words, the functional square root of a function g is a function f satisfying f(f(x)) = g(x) for all x. For example, f(x) = 2x2 is a functional square root of g(x) = 8x4.

a. Debt
b. Point-slope form
c. Total least squares
d. Square function


23. In mathematics, a _____ is a function whose definition is dependent on the value of the independent variable. Mathematically, a real-valued function f of a real variable x is a relationship whose definition is given differently on disjoint subsets of its domain

The word piecewise is also used to describe any property of a _____ that holds for each piece but may not hold for the whole domain of the function.

a. High-dimensional model representation
b. Glide reflection
c. Surjective
d. Piecewise-defined function


24. In mathematics, the _____ is a conic section, the intersection of a right circular conical surface and a plane parallel to a generating straight line of that surface. Given a point and a line that lie in a plane, the locus of points in that plane that are equidistant to them is a _____.

A particular case arises when the plane is tangent to the conical surface of a circle.

a. Matrix representation of conic sections
b. Parabola
c. Directrix
d. Dandelin sphere


25. A _____, in mathematics, is a polynomial function of the form $f(x) = ax^2 + bx + c$, where $a \neq 0$. The graph of a _____ is a parabola whose major axis is parallel to the y-axis.

The expression ax² + bx + c in the definition of a _____ is a polynomial of degree 2 or a 2nd degree polynomial, because the highest exponent of x is 2.

a. Discriminant
b. Multivariate division algorithm
c. Laguerre polynomials
d. Quadratic function


26. In mathematics, an _____ is a statement about the relative size or order of two objects, or about whether they are the same or not

- The notation a < b means that a is less than b.
- The notation a > b means that a is greater than b.
- The notation a ≠ b means that a is not equal to b, but does not say that one is bigger than the other or even that they can be compared in size.

In all these cases, a is not equal to b, hence, '_____'.

These relations are known as strict _____

- The notation a ≤ b means that a is less than or equal to b;
- The notation a ≥ b means that a is greater than or equal to b;

An additional use of the notation is to show that one quantity is much greater than another, normally by several orders of magnitude.

- The notation a << b means that a is much less than b.
- The notation a >> b means that a is much greater than b.

If the sense of the _____ is the same for all values of the variables for which its members are defined, then the _____ is called an 'absolute' or 'unconditional' _____. If the sense of an _____ holds only for certain values of the variables involved, but is reversed or destroyed for other values of the variables, it is called a conditional _____.

An _____ may appear unsolvable because it only states whether a number is larger or smaller than another number; but it is possible to apply the same operations for equalities to inequalities. For example, to find x for the _____ 10x > 23 one would divide 23 by 10.

a. A Mathematical Theory of Communication
b. A posteriori
c. Inequality
d. A chemical equation

27. _____ is an algebraic technique used to solve quadratic equations, in analytic geometry for determining the shapes of graphs, and in calculus for computing integrals. The essential objective is to reduce a quadratic polynomial in a variable in an equation or expression to a squared polynomial of linear order. This can reduce an equation or integral to one that is more easily solved or evaluated.
   a. Completing the square
   b. Monomial basis
   c. Permanent of a matrix
   d. Relation algebra


28. _____, also sometimes known as standard form or as exponential notation, is a way of writing numbers that accommodates values too large or small to be conveniently written in standard decimal notation. _____ has a number of useful properties and is often favored by scientists, mathematicians and engineers, who work with such numbers.

In _____, numbers are written in the form:

$$a \times 10^b$$

   a. Radix point
   b. Leading zero
   c. 1-center problem
   d. Scientific notation


29. In geometry, a _____ is a special kind of point, usually a corner of a polygon, polyhedron, or higher dimensional polytope. In the geometry of curves a _____ is a point of where the first derivative of curvature is zero. In graph theory, a _____ is the fundamental unit out of which graphs are formed
   a. Duality
   b. Vertex
   c. Crib
   d. Dini


30. In economics, specifically cost accounting, the _____ is the point at which cost or expenses and revenue are equal: there is no net loss or gain, and one has 'broken even'. Therefore has not made a profit or a loss.

In the linear Cost-Volume-Profit Analysis model, the _____ can be directly computed in terms of Total Revenue and Total Costs as:

$$TR = TC$$
$$P \times X = TFC + V \times X$$
$$P \times X - V \times X = TFC$$
$$(P - V) \times X = TFC$$
$$X = \frac{TFC}{P - V}$$

where:

- TFC is Total Fixed Costs,
- P is Unit Sale Price, and
- V is Unit Variable Cost.

The _____ can alternatively be computed as the point where Contribution equals Fixed Costs.

The quantity $(P - V)$ is of interest in its own right, and is called the Unit Contribution Margin: it is the marginal profit per unit, or alternatively the portion of each sale that contributes to Fixed Costs. Thus the _____ can be more simply computed as the point where Total Contribution = Total Fixed Cost:

$$\text{Total Contribution} = \text{Total Fixed Costs}$$
$$\text{Unit Contribution} \times \text{Number of Units} = \text{Total Fixed Costs}$$
$$\text{Number of Units} = \frac{\text{Total Fixed Costs}}{\text{Unit Contribution}}$$

In currency units to reach break-even, one can use the above calculation and multiply by Price, or equivalently use the Contribution Margin Ratio to compute it as:

$$\text{Break-even(in Sales)} = \frac{\text{Fixed Costs}}{C/P}.$$

R=C Where R is revenue generated C is cost incurred.

a. Break-even point
b. 120-cell
c. Small numbers game
d. 1-center problem

31. In mathematics, a _____ is an expression constructed from variables and constants, using the operations of addition, subtraction, multiplication, and constant non-negative whole number exponents. For example, $x^2 - 4x + 7$ is a _____, but $x^2 - 4/x + 7x^{3/2}$ is not, because its second term involves division by the variable x and also because its third term contains an exponent that is not a whole number.

_____s are one of the most important concepts in algebra and throughout mathematics and science.

   a. Semifield
   b. Group extension
   c. Coimage
   d. Polynomial


32. In mathematics, a _____ is any function which can be written as the ratio of two polynomial functions. _____ of degree 2 :

$$y = \frac{x^2 - 3x - 2}{x^2 - 4}$$

In the case of one variable, x, a _____ is a function of the form

$$f(x) = \frac{P(x)}{Q(x)}$$

where P and Q are polynomial function in x and Q is not the zero polynomial. The domain of f is the set of all points x for which the denominator Q

   a. Legendre rational functions
   b. 1-center problem
   c. Rational function
   d. 120-cell


33. In probability theory, a probability distribution is called _____ if its cumulative distribution function is _____. That is equivalent to saying that for random variables X with the distribution in question, $Pr[X = a] = 0$ for all real numbers a. If the distribution of X is _____ then X is called a _____ random variable.

   a. Continuous
   b. Concatenated codes
   c. Continuous phase modulation
   d. Conull set

34. Suppose f is a function. Then the line y = a is a _____ for f if

$$\lim_{x \to \infty} f(x) = a \text{ or } \lim_{x \to -\infty} f(x) = a.$$

Intuitively, this means that f(x) can be made as close as desired to a by making x big enough. How big is big enough depends on how close one wishes to make f(x) to a.

    a. 2-3 heap
    b. 120-cell
    c. 1-center problem
    d. Horizontal asymptote


35. An _____ of a real-valued function y = f(x) is a curve which describes the behavior of f as either x or y tends to infinity.

In other words, as one moves along the graph of f(x) in some direction, the distance between it and the _____ eventually becomes smaller than any distance that one may specify.

If a curve A has the curve B as an _____, one says that A is asymptotic to B. Similarly B is asymptotic to A, so A and B are called asymptotic.

    a. Improper integral
    b. Infinite product
    c. Isoperimetric dimension
    d. Asymptote


36. The _____ is a function in mathematics. The application of this function to a value x is written as ex. Equivalently, this can be written in the form $e^x$, where e is a mathematical constant, the base of the natural logarithm, which equals approximately 2.718281828, and is also known as Euler's number.
    a. A chemical equation
    b. Area hyperbolic functions
    c. A Mathematical Theory of Communication
    d. Exponential function


37. In mathematics and computer science, _____ (also base-16, hexa or base, of 16. It uses sixteen distinct symbols, most often the symbols 0-9 to represent values zero to nine, and A, B, C, D, E, F (or a through f) to represent values ten to fifteen.

Its primary use is as a human friendly representation of binary coded values, so it is often used in digital electronics and computer engineering.

a. Tetradecimal
b. Hexadecimal
c. Factoradic
d. Radix



38. A _____ is a software program that facilitates symbolic mathematics. The core functionality of a CAS is manipulation of mathematical expressions in symbolic form.

The symbolic manipulations supported typically include

- simplification to the smallest possible expression or some standard form, including automatic simplification with assumptions and simplification with constraints
- substitution of symbolic, functors or numeric values for expressions
- change of form of expressions: expanding products and powers, partial and full factorization, rewriting as partial fractions, constraint satisfaction, rewriting trigonometric functions as exponentials, etc.
- partial and total differentiation
- symbolic constrained and unconstrained global optimization
- solution of linear and some non-linear equations over various domains
- solution of some differential and difference equations
- taking some limits
- some indefinite and definite integration, including multidimensional integrals
- integral transforms
- arbitrary-precision numeric operations
- Series operations such as expansion, summation and products
- matrix operations including products, inverses, etc.
- display of mathematical expressions in two-dimensional mathematical form, often using typesetting systems similar to TeX
- add-ons for use in applied mathematics such as physics packages for physical computation
- plotting graphs and parametric plots of functions in two and three dimensions, and animating them
- APIs for linking it on an external program such as a database, or using in a programming language to use the _____
- drawing charts and diagrams
- string manipulation such as matching and searching
- statistical computation
- Theorem proving and verification
- graphic production and editing such as CGI and signal processing as image processing
- sound synthesis

Many also include a programming language, allowing users to implement their own algorithms.

Some _____s focus on a specific area of application; these are typically developed in academia and are free.

a. Computer algebra system
b. 2-3 heap
c. 120-cell
d. 1-center problem

39. _____ occurs when the growth rate of a mathematical function is proportional to the function's current value. In the case of a discrete domain of definition with equal intervals it is also called geometric growth or geometric decay.

With _____ of a positive value its rate of increase steadily increases, or in the case of exponential decay, its rate of decrease steadily decreases.

a. Exponential growth
b. A Mathematical Theory of Communication
c. A posteriori
d. A chemical equation

40. The _____ fallacy is an informal fallacy. It ascribes cause where none exists. The flaw is failing to account for natural fluctuations.

a. Differential
b. Depth
c. Degrees of freedom
d. Regression

41. _____ is the concept of adding accumulated interest back to the principal, so that interest is earned on interest from that moment on. The act of declaring interest to be principal is called compounding. A loan, for example, may have its interest compounded every month: in this case, a loan with $100 principal and 1% interest per month would have a balance of $101 at the end of the first month.

a. Compound interest
b. Net interest margin securities
c. Retained interest
d. Net interest margin

## Chapter 2. Functions and Graphs

42. _____ is a fee, paid on borrowed capital. Assets lent include money, shares, consumer goods through hire purchase, major assets such as aircraft, and even entire factories in finance lease arrangements. The _____ is calculated upon the value of the assets in the same manner as upon money.
    a. Interest
    b. Interest expense
    c. A Mathematical Theory of Communication
    d. Interest sensitivity gap

43. In mathematics and in the sciences, a _____ (plural: _____ e, formulæ or _____ s) is a concise way of expressing information symbolically (as in a mathematical or chemical _____), or a general relationship between quantities. One of many famous _____ e is Albert Einstein's $E = mc^2$ (see special relativity

    In mathematics, a _____ is a key to solve an equation with variables. For example, the problem of determining the volume of a sphere is one that requires a significant amount of integral calculus to solve.

    a. 120-cell
    b. 1-center problem
    c. 2-3 heap
    d. Formula

44. The function $\log_b(x)$ depends on both b and x, but the term _____ (or logarithmic function) in standard usage refers to a function of the form $\log_b(x)$ in which the base b is fixed and so the only argument is x. Thus there is one _____ for each value of the base b (which must be positive and must differ from 1.) Viewed in this way, the base-b _____ is the inverse function of the exponential function $b^x$.
    a. 120-cell
    b. 1-center problem
    c. 2-3 heap
    d. Logarithm function

45. In mathematics, the _____ of a number n is the number that, when added to n, yields zero. The _____ of n is denoted −n. For example, 7 is −7, because 7 + (−7) = 0, and the _____ of −0.3 is 0.3, because −0.3 + 0.3 = 0.
    a. Additive inverse
    b. Associativity
    c. Algebraic structure
    d. Arity

46. An _____ is a function which does the reverse of a given function.

a. A Mathematical Theory of Communication
b. Empty set
c. Inverse function
d. Empty function

47. An injective function is called an injection, and is also said to be a _____ (not to be confused with one-to-one correspondence, i.e. a bijective function.)

A function f that is not injective is sometimes called many-to-one. (However, this terminology is also sometimes used to mean 'single-valued', i.e. each argument is mapped to at most one value.)

a. A posteriori
b. One-to-one function
c. A Mathematical Theory of Communication
d. A chemical equation

48. In statistics the _____ of an event i is the number $n_i$ of times the event occurred in the experiment or the study. These frequencies are often graphically represented in histograms.

We speak of absolute frequencies, when the counts $n_i$ themselves are given and of

$$f_i = \frac{n_i}{N} = \frac{n_i}{\sum_i n_i}$$

Taking the $f_i$ for all i and tabulating or plotting them leads to a _____ distribution.

a. Subharmonic
b. Frequency
c. Digital room correction
d. Robinson-Dadson curves

49. In geometry a _____ is traditionally a plane figure that is bounded by a closed path or circuit, composed of a finite sequence of straight line segments. These segments are called its edges or sides, and the points where two edges meet are the _____'s vertices or corners. The interior of the _____ is sometimes called its body.

## Chapter 2. Functions and Graphs

a. Polygon
b. Parallelogon
c. Polygonal curve
d. Regular polygon

50. _____ are used in computer graphics to compose images that are three-dimensional in appearance. Usually triangular, _____ arise when an object's surface is modeled, vertices are selected, and the object is rendered in a wire frame model. This is quicker to display than a shaded model; thus the _____ are a stage in computer animation.
   a. Heptadecagon
   b. Visibility polygon
   c. Polygons
   d. Triskaidecagon

51. A _____ is a device for performing mathematical calculations, distinguished from a computer by having a limited problem solving ability and an interface optimized for interactive calculation rather than programming. _____s can be hardware or software, and mechanical or electronic, and are often built into devices such as PDAs or mobile phones.

Modern electronic _____s are generally small, digital, and usually inexpensive.

   a. Calculator
   b. 2-3 heap
   c. 120-cell
   d. 1-center problem

52. The _____ is the logarithm with base 10. It is also known as the decadic logarithm, named after its base. It is indicated by $\log_{10}$
   a. 1-center problem
   b. Logarithmic growth
   c. Natural logarithm
   d. Common logarithm

53. In mathematics, the _____ of a number to a given base is the power or exponent to which the base must be raised in order to produce the number.

For example, the _____ of 1000 to the base 10 is 3, because 3 is how many 10s one must multiply to get 1000: thus 10 × 10 × 10 = 1000; the base-2 _____ of 32 is 5 because 5 is how many 2s one must multiply to get 32: thus 2 × 2 × 2 × 2 × 2 = 32. In the language of exponents: $10^3$ = 1000, so $\log_{10} 1000$ = 3, and $2^5$ = 32, so $\log_2 32$ = 5.

   a. 120-cell
   b. 2-3 heap
   c. 1-center problem
   d. Logarithm


54. The _____, formerly known as the hyperbolic logarithm, is the logarithm to the base e, where e is an irrational constant approximately equal to 2.718 281 828. It is also sometimes referred to as the Napierian logarithm, although the original meaning of this term is slightly different. In simple terms, the _____ of a number x is the power to which e would have to be raised to equal x -- for example the natural log of e itself is 1 because $e^1$ = e, while the _____ of 1 would be 0, since $e^0$ = 1.
   a. Logarithmic growth
   b. 1-center problem
   c. Natural logarithm
   d. Logarithmic identities


55. The _____ is the period of time required for a quantity to double in size or value.
   a. Zenzizenzizenzic
   b. Power law
   c. Doubling time
   d. Stretched exponential function


56. In computational complexity theory, an algorithm is said to take _____ if the asymptotic upper bound for the time it requires is proportional to the size of the input, which is usually denoted n.

Informally spoken, the running time increases linearly with the size of the input. For example, a procedure that adds up all elements of a list requires time proportional to the length of the list.

   a. Time-constructible function
   b. Truth table reduction
   c. Constructible function
   d. Linear time

## Chapter 3. Mathematics of Finance

1. In abstract algebra, a module S over a ring R is called _____ or irreducible if it is not the zero module 0 and if its only submodules are 0 and S. Understanding the _____ modules over a ring is usually helpful because these modules form the 'building blocks' of all other modules in a certain sense.

Abelian groups are the same as Z-modules.

   a. Harmonic series
   b. Basis
   c. Simple
   d. Derivation


2. In mathematics, _____ and undefined are used to explain whether or not expressions have meaningful, sensible, and unambiguous values. Not all branches of mathematics come to the same conclusion.

The following expressions are undefined in all contexts, but remarks in the analysis section may apply.

   a. Defined
   b. Plugging in
   c. Toy model
   d. LHS


3. In mathematics and in the sciences, a _____ (plural: _____e, formulæ or _____s) is a concise way of expressing information symbolically (as in a mathematical or chemical _____), or a general relationship between quantities. One of many famous _____e is Albert Einstein's E = mc² (see special relativity

In mathematics, a _____ is a key to solve an equation with variables. For example, the problem of determining the volume of a sphere is one that requires a significant amount of integral calculus to solve.

   a. 120-cell
   b. 2-3 heap
   c. Formula
   d. 1-center problem


4. _____ is a fee, paid on borrowed capital. Assets lent include money, shares, consumer goods through hire purchase, major assets such as aircraft, and even entire factories in finance lease arrangements. The _____ is calculated upon the value of the assets in the same manner as upon money.

a. A Mathematical Theory of Communication
b. Interest
c. Interest sensitivity gap
d. Interest expense


5. In mathematics, hyperbolic n-space, denoted $H^n$, is the maximally symmetric, simply connected, n-dimensional Riemannian manifold with constant sectional curvature −1. _____ is the principal example of a space exhibiting hyperbolic geometry. It can be thought of as the negative-curvature analogue of the n-sphere.
   a. Margulis lemma
   b. Hyperbolic geometry
   c. Horocycle
   d. Hyperbolic space


6. _____ is the concept of adding accumulated interest back to the principal, so that interest is earned on interest from that moment on. The act of declaring interest to be principal is called compounding. A loan, for example, may have its interest compounded every month: in this case, a loan with $100 principal and 1% interest per month would have a balance of $101 at the end of the first month.
   a. Retained interest
   b. Net interest margin
   c. Net interest margin securities
   d. Compound interest


7. In probability theory, a probability distribution is called _____ if its cumulative distribution function is _____. That is equivalent to saying that for random variables X with the distribution in question, Pr[X = a] = 0 for all real numbers a. If the distribution of X is _____ then X is called a _____ random variable.
   a. Continuous
   b. Continuous phase modulation
   c. Concatenated codes
   d. Conull set


8. In mathematics, a _____ is a number that can be expressed as an integral of an algebraic function over an algebraic domain. Kontsevich and Zagier define a _____ as a complex number whose real and imaginary parts are values of absolutely convergent integrals of rational functions with rational coefficients, over domains in given by polynomial inequalities with rational coefficients.

## Chapter 3. Mathematics of Finance

a. Closeness
b. Boussinesq approximation
c. Period
d. Disk


9. _____ is an English dubstep/electronic music duo formed in 2003. The group blends samples, acoustic and electronic instrumentation, and singing from a revolving cast of vocalists. Its members, Adam and Ian, purposefully give very little information about the group or themselves, and tend to do little in the way of self-promotion.

a. 120-cell
b. 2-3 heap
c. Various
d. 1-center problem


10. A _____ typically refers to a class of handheld calculators that are capable of plotting graphs, solving simultaneous equations, and performing numerous other tasks with variables. Most popular _____s are also programmable, allowing the user to create customized programs, typically for scientific/engineering and education applications. Due to their large displays intended for graphing, they can also accommodate several lines of text and calculations at a time.

a. Genus
b. Support vector machines
c. Bump mapping
d. Graphing calculator


11. A _____ is a device for performing mathematical calculations, distinguished from a computer by having a limited problem solving ability and an interface optimized for interactive calculation rather than programming. _____s can be hardware or software, and mechanical or electronic, and are often built into devices such as PDAs or mobile phones.

Modern electronic _____s are generally small, digital, and usually inexpensive.

a. 120-cell
b. 1-center problem
c. 2-3 heap
d. Calculator


12. _____ is usually defined as the activity of using and developing computer technology, computer hardware and software. It is the computer-specific part of information technology. Computer science (or _____ science) is the study and the science of the theoretical foundations of information and computation and their implementation and application in computer systems.

a. Computing
b. Deterministic finite state machine
c. Parallel Random Access Machine
d. Probabilistic Turing Machine


13.   In computational complexity theory, an algorithm is said to take _____ if the asymptotic upper bound for the time it requires is proportional to the size of the input, which is usually denoted n.

Informally spoken, the running time increases linearly with the size of the input. For example, a procedure that adds up all elements of a list requires time proportional to the length of the list.

a. Constructible function
b. Linear time
c. Time-constructible function
d. Truth table reduction


14.   _____ expresses an annual rate of interest taking into account the effect of compounding, usually for deposit or investment products. It is analogous to the Annual percentage rate, which is used for loans. In some jurisdictions, the use and definition of _____ may be regulated by a government agency, in which case it would generally be capitalized.

a. A chemical equation
b. Annual percentage yield
c. A Mathematical Theory of Communication
d. A posteriori


15.   In mathematics, a _____ is a way of expressing a number as a fraction of 100. It is often denoted using the percent sign, '%'. For example, 45% is equal to 45 / 100, or 0.45.

a. Subtrahend
b. Lowest common denominator
c. Percentage
d. Least common multiple


16.   The term _____ refers to the central sense organ complex, for those animals that have one, normally on the ventral surface of the head and can depending on the definition in the human case, include the hair, forehead, eyebrow, eyes, nose, ears, cheeks, mouth, lips, philtrum, teeth, skin, and chin. The _____ has uses of expression, appearance, and identity amongst others.It also has different senses like smelling, tasting, hearing, and seeing.

## Chapter 3. Mathematics of Finance

Caricatures often exaggerate facial features to make a _____ more easily recognized in association with a pronounced portion of the _____ of the individual in question--for example, a caricature of Osama bin Laden might focus on his facial hair and nose; a caricature of George W. Bush might enlarge his ears to the size of an elephant¢s; a caricature of Jay Leno may pronounce his head and chin; and a caricature of Mick Jagger might enlarge his lips.

a. 1-center problem
b. 2-3 heap
c. 120-cell
d. Face


17. In financial accounting, a _____ or statement of financial position is a summary of a person's or organization's balances. Assets, liabilities and ownership equity are listed as of a specific date, such as the end of its financial year. A _____ is often described as a snapshot of a company's financial condition.

a. 1-center problem
b. 120-cell
c. 2-3 heap
d. Balance sheet


18. _____ or amortisation is the process of decreasing an amount over a period of time. The word comes from Middle English amortisen to kill, alienate in mortmain, from Anglo-French amorteser, alteration of amortir, from Vulgar Latin admortire to kill, from Latin ad- + mort-, mors death. Particular instances of the term include:

- _____, the allocation of a lump sum amount to different time periods, particularly for loans and other forms of finance, including related interest or other finance charges.
    - _____ schedule, a table detailing each periodic payment on a loan, as generated by an _____ calculator.
    - Negative _____, an _____ schedule where the loan amount actually increases through not paying the full interest
- Amortized analysis, analyzing the execution cost of algorithms over a sequence of operations.
- _____ of capital expenditures of certain assets under accounting rules, particularly intangible assets, in a manner analogous to depreciation.
- _____

_____ is also used in the context of zoning regulations and describes the time in which a property owner has to relocate when the property's use constitutes a preexisting nonconforming use under zoning regulations.

- Depreciation

a. ISAAC
b. Origin
c. Identity
d. Amortization

19. _____ is that which is owed; usually referencing assets owed, but the term can cover other obligations. In the case of assets, _____ is a means of using future purchasing power in the present before a summation has been earned.

a. Metaheuristic
b. Debt
c. Cobb-Douglas
d. Point-slope form

20. An _____ is a table detailing each periodic payment on a amortizing loan, as generated by an amortization calculator.

While a portion of every payment is applied towards both the interest and the principal balance of the loan, the exact amount applied to principal each time varies. An _____ reveals the specific monetary amount put towards interest, as well as the specific put towards the Principal balance, with each payment.

a. Amortization schedule
b. A chemical equation
c. Accounts receivable
d. A Mathematical Theory of Communication

21. _____ is the concept or idea of fairness in economics, particularly as to taxation or welfare economics.
a. Union
b. Event
c. Interval
d. Equity

22. In game theory, a player's _____ in a game is a complete plan of action for whatever situation might arise; this fully determines the player's behaviour. A player's _____ will determine the action the player will take at any stage of the game, for every possible history of play up to that stage.

A _____ profile is a set of strategies for each player which fully specifies all actions in a game.

a. Strategy
b. Correlated equilibrium
c. Matching pennies
d. Sir Philip Sidney game

## Chapter 4. Systems of Linear Equations; Matrices

1. In linear algebra, the _____ of a matrix is obtained by changing a matrix in some way.

Given the matrices A and B, where:

$$A = \begin{bmatrix} 1 & 3 & 2 \\ 2 & 0 & 1 \\ 5 & 2 & 2 \end{bmatrix}, \quad B = \begin{bmatrix} 4 \\ 3 \\ 1 \end{bmatrix}$$

Then, the _____ is written as:

$$(A|B) = \begin{bmatrix} 1 & 3 & 2 & 4 \\ 2 & 0 & 1 & 3 \\ 5 & 2 & 2 & 1 \end{bmatrix}$$

This is useful when solving systems of linear equations or the _____ may also be used to find the inverse of a matrix by combining it with the identity matrix.

$$C = \begin{bmatrix} 1 & 3 \\ -5 & 0 \end{bmatrix}$$

Let C be a square 2×2 matrix where

To find the inverse of C we create where I is the 2×2 identity matrix.

a. Augmented matrix
b. Alternating sign matrix
c. Eigendecomposition
d. Unimodular polynomial matrix


2. A _____ is an algebraic equation in which each term is either a constant or the product of a constant and a single variable. _____s can have one, two, three or more variables.

_____s occur with great regularity in applied mathematics.

a. Difference of two squares
b. Quadratic equation
c. Quartic equation
d. Linear equation


3. _____ is a branch of mathematics which focuses on the study of matrices. Initially a sub-branch of linear algebra, it has grown to cover subjects related to graph theory, algebra, combinatorics, and statistics as well.

## Chapter 4. Systems of Linear Equations; Matrices

The term matrix was first coined in 1848 by J.J. Sylvester as a name of an array of numbers.

a. Segre classification
b. Semi-simple operators
c. Pairing
d. Matrix theory



4. In mathematics, a _____ is a rectangular table of elements, which may be numbers or, more generally, any abstract quantities that can be added and multiplied. Matrices are used to describe linear equations, keep track of the coefficients of linear transformations and to record data that depend on multiple parameters. Matrices are described by the field of _____ theory.

a. Coherent
b. Double counting
c. Compression
d. Matrix



5. In logic, a theory is _____ if it does not contain a contradiction. The lack of contradiction can be defined in either semantic or syntactic terms. The semantic definition states that a theory is _____ if it has a model; this is the sense used in traditional Aristotelian logic, although in contemporary mathematical logic the term satisfiable is used instead.

a. Second-order logic
b. First-order logic
c. Consistent
d. Logic



6. In the study of metric spaces in mathematics, there are various notions of two metrics on the same underlying space being 'the same', or _____.

In the following, M will denote a non-empty set and $d_1$ and $d_2$ will denote two metrics on M.

The two metrics $d_1$ and $d_2$ are said to be topologically _____ if they generate the same topology on M.

a. A Mathematical Theory of Communication
b. A chemical equation
c. A posteriori
d. Equivalent

## Chapter 4. Systems of Linear Equations; Matrices

7. A _____ is a device for performing mathematical calculations, distinguished from a computer by having a limited problem solving ability and an interface optimized for interactive calculation rather than programming. _____s can be hardware or software, and mechanical or electronic, and are often built into devices such as PDAs or mobile phones.

Modern electronic _____s are generally small, digital, and usually inexpensive.

  a. 120-cell
  b. 2-3 heap
  c. 1-center problem
  d. Calculator

8. A _____ typically refers to a class of handheld calculators that are capable of plotting graphs, solving simultaneous equations, and performing numerous other tasks with variables. Most popular _____s are also programmable, allowing the user to create customized programs, typically for scientific/engineering and education applications. Due to their large displays intended for graphing, they can also accommodate several lines of text and calculations at a time.
  a. Support vector machines
  b. Genus
  c. Bump mapping
  d. Graphing calculator

9. In mathematics, the point $\tilde{\mathbf{x}} \in \mathbb{R}^n$ is an _____ for the differential equation

$$\frac{d\mathbf{x}}{dt} = \mathbf{f}(t, \mathbf{x})$$

if $\mathbf{f}(t, \tilde{\mathbf{x}}) = 0$ for all $t$.

Similarly, the point $\tilde{\mathbf{x}} \in \mathbb{R}^n$ is an _____ for the difference equation

$$\mathbf{x}_{k+1} = \mathbf{f}(k, \mathbf{x}_k)$$

if $\mathbf{f}(k, \tilde{\mathbf{x}}) = \tilde{\mathbf{x}}$ for $k = 0, 1, 2, \ldots$.

Equilibria can be classified by looking at the signs of the eigenvalues of the linearization of the equations about the equilibria.

a. Algorithm design
b. Uniform algebra
c. Equilibrium point
d. Unitary transformation

10. In mathematics, an _____ or member of a set is any one of the distinct objects that make up that set.

Writing A = {1,2,3,4}, means that the _____s of the set A are the numbers 1, 2, 3 and 4. Groups of _____s of A, for example {1,2}, are subsets of A.

a. Universal code
b. Order
c. Element
d. Ideal

11. In linear algebra, a row vector or _____ is a 1 × n matrix, that is, a matrix consisting of a single row:

$$\mathbf{x} = \begin{bmatrix} x_1 & x_2 & \ldots & x_m \end{bmatrix}.$$

The transpose of a row vector is a column vector:

$$\begin{bmatrix} x_1 \\ x_2 \\ \vdots \\ x_m \end{bmatrix} = \begin{bmatrix} x_1 & x_2 & \ldots & x_m \end{bmatrix}^{\mathrm{T}}.$$

The set of all row vectors forms a vector space which is the dual space to the set of all column vectors.

Row vectors are sometimes written using the following non-standard notation:

$$\mathbf{x} = \begin{bmatrix} x_1, x_2, \ldots, x_m \end{bmatrix}.$$

- Matrix multiplication involves the action of multiplying each row vector of one matrix by each column vector of another matrix.

- The dot product of two vectors a and b is equivalent to multiplying the row vector representation of a by the column vector representation of b:

$$\mathbf{a} \cdot \mathbf{b} = \begin{bmatrix} a_1 & a_2 & a_3 \end{bmatrix} \begin{bmatrix} b_1 \\ b_2 \\ b_3 \end{bmatrix}.$$

a. Woodbury matrix identity
b. Row matrix
c. Gram-Schmidt process
d. Dual vector space

12. In linear algebra, a column vector or _____ is an m × 1 matrix, i.e. a matrix consisting of a single column of $m$ elements.

$$\mathbf{x} = \begin{bmatrix} x_1 \\ x_2 \\ \vdots \\ x_m \end{bmatrix}$$

The transpose of a column vector is a row vector and vice versa.

The set of all column vectors forms a vector space which is the dual space to the set of all row vectors.

a. Split-complex number
b. Spread of a matrix
c. Cayley-Hamilton theorem
d. Column matrix

13. In mathematics, _____ and undefined are used to explain whether or not expressions have meaningful, sensible, and unambiguous values. Not all branches of mathematics come to the same conclusion.

The following expressions are undefined in all contexts, but remarks in the analysis section may apply.

   a. Defined
   b. Toy model
   c. LHS
   d. Plugging in


14. In mathematics, an _____ in the sense of ring theory is a subring $\mathcal{O}$ of a ring R that satisfies the conditions

   1. R is a ring which is a finite-dimensional algebra over the rational number field $\mathbb{Q}$
   2. $\mathcal{O}$ spans R over $\mathbb{Q}$, so that $\mathbb{Q}\mathcal{O} = R$, and
   3. $\mathcal{O}$ is a lattice in R.

The third condition can be stated more accurately, in terms of the extension of scalars of R to the real numbers, embedding R in a real vector space. In less formal terms, additively $\mathcal{O}$ should be a free abelian group generated by a basis for R over $\mathbb{Q}$.

The leading example is the case where R is a number field K and $\mathcal{O}$ is its ring of integers. In algebraic number theory there are examples for any K other than the rational field of proper subrings of the ring of integers that are also _____s.

   a. Order
   b. Algebraic
   c. Annihilator
   d. Efficiency


15. In linear algebra, _____ is a version of Gaussian elimination that puts zeros both above and below each pivot element as it goes from the top row of the given matrix to the bottom. In other words, _____ brings a matrix to reduced row echelon form, whereas Gaussian elimination takes it only as far as row echelon form. Every matrix has a reduced row echelon form, and this algorithm is guaranteed to produce it.

   a. Conservation form
   b. Lax equivalence theorem
   c. Spheroidal wave functions
   d. Gauss-Jordan elimination

16. In linear algebra a matrix is in row echelon form if

- All nonzero rows are above any rows of all zeroes, and
- The leading coefficient of a row is always strictly to the right of the leading coefficient of the row above it.

This is the definition used in this article, but some texts add a third condition:

- The leading coefficient of each nonzero row is one.

A matrix is in _____ (also called row canonical form) if it satisfies the above three conditions, and if, in addition

- Every leading coefficient is the only nonzero entry in its column.

The first non-zero entry in each row is called a pivot.

This matrix is in _____ :

$$\begin{bmatrix} 0 & 1 & 4 & 0 & 0 \\ 0 & 0 & 0 & 1 & 0 \\ 0 & 0 & 0 & 0 & 1 \\ 0 & 0 & 0 & 0 & 0 \end{bmatrix}.$$

The following matrix is also in row echelon form, but not in reduced row form:

$$\begin{bmatrix} 1 & 1 & 1 & 1 \\ 0 & 9 & 0 & 2 \\ 0 & 0 & 0 & 3 \end{bmatrix}.$$

However, this matrix is not in row echelon form, as the leading coefficient of row 3 is not strictly to the right of the leading coefficient of row 2.

$$\begin{bmatrix} 1 & 2 & 3 & 4 \\ 0 & 3 & 7 & 2 \\ 0 & 2 & 0 & 0 \end{bmatrix}$$

Every non-zero matrix can be reduced to an infinite number of echelon forms (they can all be multiples of each other, for example) via elementary matrix transformations.

a. Pseudospectrum
b. Reduced row echelon form
c. Basic Linear Algebra Subprograms
d. Folded spectrum method

17. In linear algebra a matrix is in _____ if

    - All nonzero rows are above any rows of all zeroes, and
    - The leading coefficient of a row is always strictly to the right of the leading coefficient of the row above it.

This is the definition used in this article, but some texts add a third condition:

- The leading coefficient of each nonzero row is one.

A matrix is in reduced _____ if it satisfies the above three conditions, and if, in addition

- Every leading coefficient is the only nonzero entry in its column.

The first non-zero entry in each row is called a pivot.

This matrix is in reduced _____:

$$\begin{bmatrix} 0 & 1 & 4 & 0 & 0 \\ 0 & 0 & 0 & 1 & 0 \\ 0 & 0 & 0 & 0 & 1 \\ 0 & 0 & 0 & 0 & 0 \end{bmatrix}.$$

The following matrix is also in _____, but not in reduced row form:

$$\begin{bmatrix} 1 & 1 & 1 & 1 \\ 0 & 9 & 0 & 2 \\ 0 & 0 & 0 & 3 \end{bmatrix}.$$

However, this matrix is not in _____, as the leading coefficient of row 3 is not strictly to the right of the leading coefficient of row 2.

$$\begin{bmatrix} 1 & 2 & 3 & 4 \\ 0 & 3 & 7 & 2 \\ 0 & 2 & 0 & 0 \end{bmatrix}$$

Every non-zero matrix can be reduced to an infinite number of echelon forms via elementary matrix transformations.

a. Portable, Extensible Toolkit for Scientific Computation
b. Row echelon form
c. Reduced row echelon form
d. Gaussian elimination


18. A _____ is a deliberate process for transforming one or more inputs into one or more results, with variable change.

The term is used in a variety of senses, from the very definite arithmetical using an algorithm to the vague heuristics of calculating a strategy in a competition or calculating the chance of a successful relationship between two people.

Multiplying 7 by 8 is a simple algorithmic _____.

a. Mathematical object
b. Mathematics Subject Classification
c. Mathematical maturity
d. Calculation


19. _____ is the mathematical operation of scaling one number by another. It is one of the four basic operations in elementary arithmetic.

_____ is defined for whole numbers in terms of repeated addition; for example, 4 multiplied by 3 can be calculated by adding 3 copies of 4 together:

$$4 + 4 + 4 = 12.$$

_____ of rational numbers and real numbers is defined by systematic generalization of this basic idea.

a. The number 0 is even.
b. Highest common factor
c. Least common multiple
d. Multiplication

20. In mathematics, the term _____ has several different important meanings:

- An _____ is an equality that remains true regardless of the values of any variables that appear within it, to distinguish it from an equality which is true under more particular conditions. For this, the 'triple bar' symbol ≡ is sometimes used.
- In algebra, an _____ or _____ element of a set S with a binary operation Â· is an element e that, when combined with any element x of S, produces that same x. That is, eÂ·x = xÂ·e = x for all x in S.
    - The _____ function from a set S to itself, often denoted id or id$_S$, s the function such that i = x for all x in S. This function serves as the _____ element in the set of all functions from S to itself with respect to function composition.
    - In linear algebra, the _____ matrix of size n is the n-by-n square matrix with ones on the main diagonal and zeros elsewhere. This matrix serves as the _____ with respect to matrix multiplication.

A common example of the first meaning is the trigonometric _____

$$\sin^2 \theta + \cos^2 \theta = 1$$

which is true for all real values of θ, as opposed to

$$\cos \theta = 1,$$

which is true only for some values of θ, not all. For example, the latter equation is true when $\theta = 0$, false when $\theta = 2$

The concepts of 'additive _____' and 'multiplicative _____' are central to the Peano axioms. The number 0 is the 'additive _____' for integers, real numbers, and complex numbers. For the real numbers, for all $a \in \mathbb{R}$,

$$0 + a = a,$$

$$a + 0 = a, \text{ and}$$

$$0 + 0 = 0.$$

Similarly, The number 1 is the 'multiplicative _____' for integers, real numbers, and complex numbers.

a. Intersection
b. Identity
c. Action
d. ARIA

21. In linear algebra, the _____ or unit matrix of size n is the n-by-n square matrix with ones on the main diagonal and zeros elsewhere. It is denoted by $I_n$, or simply by I if the size is immaterial or can be trivially determined by the context. (In some fields, such as quantum mechanics, the _____ is denoted by a boldface one, 1; otherwise it is identical to I.)
   a. Associativity
   b. Identity matrix
   c. Unital
   d. Arity

22. In mathematics, the _____ of a number n is the number that, when added to n, yields zero. The _____ of n is denoted −n. For example, 7 is −7, because 7 + (−7) = 0, and the _____ of −0.3 is 0.3, because −0.3 + 0.3 = 0.
   a. Arity
   b. Additive inverse
   c. Algebraic structure
   d. Associativity

23. In mathematics, a _____ for a number x, denoted by $\frac{1}{x}$ or $x^{-1}$, is a number which when multiplied by x yields the multiplicative identity, 1. The _____ of x is also called the reciprocal of x. The _____ of a fraction $p/q$ is $q/p$.
   a. Hyperbolic function
   b. Multiplicative inverse
   c. Golden function
   d. Double exponential

24. _____ is the practice and study of hiding information. In modern times, _____ is considered a branch of both mathematics and computer science, and is affiliated closely with information theory, computer security, and engineering. _____ is used in applications present in technologically advanced societies; examples include the security of ATM cards, computer passwords, and electronic commerce, which all depend on _____.
   a. CIKS-1
   b. LOKI
   c. MAGENTA
   d. Cryptography

## Chapter 4. Systems of Linear Equations; Matrices

25. In communication theory and coding theory, _____ is the process of translating received messages into codewords of a given code These methods are often used to recover messages sent over a noisy channel, such as a binary symmetric channel.
    a. Fast Folding Algorithm
    b. MUSHRA
    c. Hilbert spectrum
    d. Decoding

26. In mathematics the _____ of a set which is equipped with the operation of addition is an element which, when added to any element x in the set, yields x. One of the most familiar additive identities is the number 0 from elementary mathematics, but additive identities occur in other mathematical structures where addition is defined, such as in groups and rings.

    - The _____ familiar from elementary mathematics is zero, denoted 0. For example,

    $5 + 0 = 5 = 0 + 5.$

    - In the natural numbers N and all of its supersets, the _____ is 0. Thus for any one of these numbers n,

    $n + 0 = n = 0 + n.$

    Let N be a set which is closed under the operation of addition, denoted +. An _____ for N is any element e such that for any element n in N,

    $e + n = n = n + e.$

    a. Unit ring
    b. Additive identity
    c. Unique factorization domain
    d. Algebraically independent

27. In mathematics, _____ is a property that a binary operation can have. It means that, within an expression containing two or more of the same associative operators in a row, the order that the operations are performed does not matter as long as the sequence of the operands is not changed. That is, rearranging the parentheses in such an expression will not change its value.
    a. Idempotence
    b. Unital
    c. Algebraically closed
    d. Associativity

28. In mathematics, and in particular in abstract algebra, distributivity is a property of binary operations that generalises the _____ law from elementary algebra.
   a. Closure with a twist
   b. General linear group
   c. Distributive
   d. Permutation

29. In mathematics, a _____ is a constant multiplicative factor of a certain object. For example, in the expression $9x^2$, the _____ of $x^2$ is 9.

The object can be such things as a variable, a vector, a function, etc.

   a. Stability radius
   b. Multivariate division algorithm
   c. Fibonacci polynomials
   d. Coefficient

1. In mathematics, _____ is a technique for optimization of a linear objective function, subject to linear equality and linear inequality constraints. Informally, _____ determines the way to achieve the best outcome in a given mathematical model given some list of requirements represented as linear equations.

More formally, given a polytope, and a real-valued affine function

$$f(x_1, x_2, \ldots, x_n) = c_1 x_1 + c_2 x_2 + \cdots + c_n x_n + d$$

defined on this polytope, a _____ method will find a point in the polytope where this function has the smallest value.

a. Linear programming relaxation
b. Lin-Kernighan
c. Descent direction
d. Linear programming

2. A _____ is a software program that facilitates symbolic mathematics. The core functionality of a CAS is manipulation of mathematical expressions in symbolic form.

The symbolic manipulations supported typically include

- simplification to the smallest possible expression or some standard form, including automatic simplification with assumptions and simplification with constraints
- substitution of symbolic, functors or numeric values for expressions
- change of form of expressions: expanding products and powers, partial and full factorization, rewriting as partial fractions, constraint satisfaction, rewriting trigonometric functions as exponentials, etc.
- partial and total differentiation
- symbolic constrained and unconstrained global optimization
- solution of linear and some non-linear equations over various domains
- solution of some differential and difference equations
- taking some limits
- some indefinite and definite integration, including multidimensional integrals
- integral transforms
- arbitrary-precision numeric operations
- Series operations such as expansion, summation and products
- matrix operations including products, inverses, etc.
- display of mathematical expressions in two-dimensional mathematical form, often using typesetting systems similar to TeX
- add-ons for use in applied mathematics such as physics packages for physical computation
- plotting graphs and parametric plots of functions in two and three dimensions, and animating them
- APIs for linking it on an external program such as a database, or using in a programming language to use the _____
- drawing charts and diagrams
- string manipulation such as matching and searching
- statistical computation
- Theorem proving and verification
- graphic production and editing such as CGI and signal processing as image processing
- sound synthesis

Many also include a programming language, allowing users to implement their own algorithms.

Some _____s focus on a specific area of application; these are typically developed in academia and are free.

a. 1-center problem
b. 2-3 heap
c. Computer algebra system
d. 120-cell


3. In mathematics, _____ and undefined are used to explain whether or not expressions have meaningful, sensible, and unambiguous values. Not all branches of mathematics come to the same conclusion.

The following expressions are undefined in all contexts, but remarks in the analysis section may apply.

a. Toy model
b. Plugging in
c. LHS
d. Defined


4. In topology, the _____ of a subset S of a topological space X is the set of points which can be approached both from S and from the outside of S. More formally, it is the set of points in the closure of S, not belonging to the interior of S. An element of the _____ of S is called a _____ point of S.
   a. Character
   b. Heap
   c. Bertrand paradox
   d. Boundary


5. _____ is either of the two parts into which a plane divides the three-dimensional space. More generally, a _____ is either of the two parts into which a hyperplane divides an affine space.
   a. Parallelogram law
   b. Simple polytope
   c. Half-space
   d. Pendent


6. In mathematics, the _____ H is the set of complex numbers

$$\mathbb{H} = \{x + iy \mid y < 0; x, y \in \mathbb{R}\}$$

with positive imaginary part y. Other names are hyperbolic plane, Poincaré plane and Lobachevsky plane, particularly in texts by Russian authors. Some authors prefer the symbol $\mathfrak{h}$.

- Upper half-plane
- Cusp neighborhood
- Fuchsian group
- Fundamental domain
- Hyperbolic geometry
- Kleinian group
- Modular group
- Poincaré metric
- Riemann surface
- Schwarz-Ahlfors-Pick theorem


a. Lower half-plane
b. Cauchy-Hadamard theorem
c. Principal branch
d. Bieberbach conjecture



7. In mathematics, the _____ H is the set of complex numbers

$$\mathbb{H} = \{x + iy \,|\, y > 0; x, y \in \mathbb{R}\}$$

with positive imaginary part y.

The term is associated with a common visualization of complex numbers with points in the plane endowed with Cartesian coordinates, with the Y-axis pointing upwards: the '_____' corresponds to the half-plane above the X-axis.

When endowed with a particular metric, the _____ may be called the hyperbolic plane, Poincaré half-plane, or Lobachevsky plane, particularly in texts by Russian authors.

a. Argument principle
b. Analytic capacity
c. Analytic continuation
d. Upper half-plane

## Chapter 5. Linear Inequalities and Linear Programming

8. In mathematics, an _____ is a statement about the relative size or order of two objects, or about whether they are the same or not

- The notation a < b means that a is less than b.
- The notation a > b means that a is greater than b.
- The notation a ≠ b means that a is not equal to b, but does not say that one is bigger than the other or even that they can be compared in size.

In all these cases, a is not equal to b, hence, '_____'.

These relations are known as strict _____

- The notation a ≤ b means that a is less than or equal to b;
- The notation a ≥ b means that a is greater than or equal to b;

An additional use of the notation is to show that one quantity is much greater than another, normally by several orders of magnitude.

- The notation a << b means that a is much less than b.
- The notation a >> b means that a is much greater than b.

If the sense of the _____ is the same for all values of the variables for which its members are defined, then the _____ is called an 'absolute' or 'unconditional' _____. If the sense of an _____ holds only for certain values of the variables involved, but is reversed or destroyed for other values of the variables, it is called a conditional _____.

An _____ may appear unsolvable because it only states whether a number is larger or smaller than another number; but it is possible to apply the same operations for equalities to inequalities. For example, to find x for the _____ 10x > 23 one would divide 23 by 10.

a. A chemical equation
b. Inequality
c. A posteriori
d. A Mathematical Theory of Communication


9. A _____ is an algebraic equation in which each term is either a constant or the product of a constant and a single variable. _____s can have one, two, three or more variables.

_____s occur with great regularity in applied mathematics.

a. Difference of two squares
b. Quartic equation
c. Linear equation
d. Quadratic equation

10. A set S of real numbers is called _____ from above if there is a real number k such that k ≥ s for all s in S. The number k is called an upper bound of S. The terms _____ from below and lower bound are similarly defined.
   a. Descent
   b. Harmonic series
   c. Derivative algebra
   d. Bounded

11. In optimization, a candidate solution is a member of a set of possible solutions to a given problem. A candidate solution does not have to be a likely or reasonable solution to the problem. The space of all candidate solutions is called the _____, feasible set, search space, or solution space.
   a. Quadratic eigenvalue problem
   b. Step response
   c. Leapfrog integration
   d. Feasible region

12. An _____ is a tree data structure in which each internal node has up to eight children. _____s are most often used to partition a three dimensional space by recursively subdividing it into eight octants. _____s are the three-dimensional analog of quadtrees.
   a. External node
   b. Adaptive k-d tree
   c. Interval tree
   d. Octree

13. In mathematics, a _____ is a condition that a solution to an optimization problem must satisfy. There are two types of _____s: equality _____s and inequality _____s. The set of solutions that satisfy all _____s is called the feasible set.
   a. Constraint
   b. Foci
   c. Concurrent
   d. Decidable

## Chapter 5. Linear Inequalities and Linear Programming

14. The mathematical concept of a _____ expresses the intuitive idea of deterministic dependence between two quantities, one of which is viewed as primary and the other as secondary. A _____ then is a way to associate a unique output for each input of a specified type, for example, a real number or an element of a given set.

   a. Grill
   b. Function
   c. Coherent
   d. Going up

15. _____ is an economics theory, that refers to individuals or societies gaining the maximum amount out of the resources they have available to them. The theory proposed by most economists is that _____ refers to the _____ of profit.

As some economists have begun to find out, this theory does not hold true for all people and cultures.

   a. Composite
   b. Maximization
   c. Homogeneity
   d. Boundary

16. In mathematics and computer science, an optimization problem is the problem of finding the best solution from all feasible solutions. More formally, an optimization problem A is a quadruple , where

   - I is a set of instances;
   - given an instance $\boxed{\times}$>, f is the set of feasible solutions;
   - given an instance x and a feasible solution y of x, m denotes the measure of y, which is usually a positive real.
   - g is the goal function, and is either min or max.

The goal is then to find for some instance x an _____, that is, a feasible solution y with

$\boxed{\times}$>

For each optimization problem, there is a corresponding decision problem that asks whether there is a feasible solution for some particular measure $m_0$. For example, if there is a graph G which contains vertices u and v, an optimization problem might be 'find a path from u to v that uses the fewest edges'. This problem might have an answer of, say, 4.

a. Optimal solution
b. Exponential time
c. Interactive proof system
d. Approximation algorithms

17. In mathematics, a _____ is a statement that can be proved on the basis of explicitly stated or previously agreed assumptions.
a. Theorem
b. Disjunction introduction
c. Logical value
d. Boolean function

## Chapter 6. Linear Programming: Simplex Method

1. In mathematics, _____ is a technique for optimization of a linear objective function, subject to linear equality and linear inequality constraints. Informally, _____ determines the way to achieve the best outcome in a given mathematical model given some list of requirements represented as linear equations.

More formally, given a polytope, and a real-valued affine function

$$f(x_1, x_2, \ldots, x_n) = c_1 x_1 + c_2 x_2 + \cdots + c_n x_n + d$$

defined on this polytope, a _____ method will find a point in the polytope where this function has the smallest value.

   a. Descent direction
   b. Linear programming
   c. Lin-Kernighan
   d. Linear programming relaxation


2. In geometry, a _____ or n-_____ is an n-dimensional analogue of a triangle. Specifically, a _____ is the convex hull of a set of affinely independent points in some Euclidean space of dimension n or higher.

For example, a 0-_____ is a point, a 1-_____ is a line segment, a 2-_____ is a triangle, a 3-_____ is a tetrahedron, and a 4-_____ is a pentachoron.

   a. Polytetrahedron
   b. Demihypercubes
   c. Simplex
   d. Hypercell


3. In mathematical optimization theory, the simplex algorithm, created by the American mathematician George Dantzig in 1947, is a popular algorithm for numerical solution of the linear programming problem. The journal Computing in Science and Engineering listed it as one of the top 10 algorithms of the century.

An unrelated, but similarly named method is the Nelder-Mead method or downhill _____ due to Nelder ' Mead and is a numerical method for optimising many-dimensional unconstrained problems, belonging to the more general class of search algorithms.

   a. Hill climbing
   b. Simplex method
   c. Fibonacci search
   d. Differential evolution

## Chapter 6. Linear Programming: Simplex Method

4. A _____ is a software program that facilitates symbolic mathematics. The core functionality of a CAS is manipulation of mathematical expressions in symbolic form.

The symbolic manipulations supported typically include

- simplification to the smallest possible expression or some standard form, including automatic simplification with assumptions and simplification with constraints
- substitution of symbolic, functors or numeric values for expressions
- change of form of expressions: expanding products and powers, partial and full factorization, rewriting as partial fractions, constraint satisfaction, rewriting trigonometric functions as exponentials, etc.
- partial and total differentiation
- symbolic constrained and unconstrained global optimization
- solution of linear and some non-linear equations over various domains
- solution of some differential and difference equations
- taking some limits
- some indefinite and definite integration, including multidimensional integrals
- integral transforms
- arbitrary-precision numeric operations
- Series operations such as expansion, summation and products
- matrix operations including products, inverses, etc.
- display of mathematical expressions in two-dimensional mathematical form, often using typesetting systems similar to TeX
- add-ons for use in applied mathematics such as physics packages for physical computation
- plotting graphs and parametric plots of functions in two and three dimensions, and animating them
- APIs for linking it on an external program such as a database, or using in a programming language to use the _____
- drawing charts and diagrams
- string manipulation such as matching and searching
- statistical computation
- Theorem proving and verification
- graphic production and editing such as CGI and signal processing as image processing
- sound synthesis

Many also include a programming language, allowing users to implement their own algorithms.

Some _____s focus on a specific area of application; these are typically developed in academia and are free.

a. 1-center problem
b. 2-3 heap
c. Computer algebra system
d. 120-cell

## Chapter 6. Linear Programming: Simplex Method

5. In mathematics, _____ and undefined are used to explain whether or not expressions have meaningful, sensible, and unambiguous values. Not all branches of mathematics come to the same conclusion.

The following expressions are undefined in all contexts, but remarks in the analysis section may apply.

a. Defined
b. Toy model
c. LHS
d. Plugging in


6. _____ is an economics theory, that refers to individuals or societies gaining the maximum amount out of the resources they have available to them. The theory proposed by most economists is that _____ refers to the _____ of profit.

As some economists have begun to find out, this theory does not hold true for all people and cultures.

a. Boundary
b. Composite
c. Homogeneity
d. Maximization


7. _____, also sometimes known as standard form or as exponential notation, is a way of writing numbers that accommodates values too large or small to be conveniently written in standard decimal notation. _____ has a number of useful properties and is often favored by scientists, mathematicians and engineers, who work with such numbers.

In _____, numbers are written in the form:

$$a \times 10^b$$

a. 1-center problem
b. Radix point
c. Scientific notation
d. Leading zero


8. In Linear programming a _____ is a variable which is added to a constraint to turn the inequality into an equation. This is required to turn an inequality into an equality where a linear combination of variables is less than or equal to a given constant in the former. As with the other variables in the augmented constraints, the _____ cannot take on negative values, as the Simplex algorithm requires them to be positive or zero.

a. Shape optimization
b. Slack variable
c. Bellman equation
d. Shekel function

9. In optimization, a candidate solution is a member of a set of possible solutions to a given problem. A candidate solution does not have to be a likely or reasonable solution to the problem. The space of all candidate solutions is called the _____, feasible set, search space, or solution space.
   a. Leapfrog integration
   b. Step response
   c. Feasible region
   d. Quadratic eigenvalue problem

10. In mathematics, a _____ is a statement that can be proved on the basis of explicitly stated or previously agreed assumptions.
    a. Boolean function
    b. Disjunction introduction
    c. Theorem
    d. Logical value

11. Initial objects are also called _____, and terminal objects are also called final.
    a. Terminal object
    b. Colimit
    c. Direct limit
    d. Coterminal

12. In mathematics, a _____ is a condition that a solution to an optimization problem must satisfy. There are two types of _____s: equality _____s and inequality _____s. The set of solutions that satisfy all _____s is called the feasible set.
    a. Constraint
    b. Foci
    c. Concurrent
    d. Decidable

13. In mathematical optimization theory, the _____, created by the North American mathematician George Dantzig in 1947, is a popular technique for numerical solution of the linear programming problem.

## Chapter 6. Linear Programming: Simplex Method

a. Sociable number
b. Partition
c. Feit–Thompson theorem
d. Simplex algorithm

14. In mathematics, an _____ or member of a set is any one of the distinct objects that make up that set.

Writing A = {1,2,3,4}, means that the _____s of the set A are the numbers 1, 2, 3 and 4. Groups of _____s of A, for example {1,2}, are subsets of A.

a. Ideal
b. Element
c. Order
d. Universal code

15. In mathematics, especially functional analysis, a hermitian element A of a C*-algebra is a _____ if its spectrum consists of nonnegative real numbers. It is possible to prove that an element x of a C*-algebra A is positive if and only if there is some b in A such that x = b*b.

If A is a bounded linear operator on a Hilbert space H, then this notion coincides with the condition that A is self-adjoint and $\langle Ax, x \rangle$ is nonnegative for every vector x in H.

a. Monotonic
b. Gelfand representation
c. Positive element
d. $C_0$-semigroup

16. In the mathematical area of order theory, every partially ordered set P gives rise to a _____ partially ordered set which is often denoted by $P^{op}$ or $P^d$. This _____ order $P^{op}$ is defined to be the set with the inverse order. It is easy to see that this construction, which can be depicted by flipping the Hasse diagram for P upside down, will indeed yield a partially ordered set.

a. Context-sensitive language
b. Christofides heuristics
c. Contraction mapping
d. Dual

## Chapter 6. Linear Programming: Simplex Method

17. In linear programming, the primary problem and the _____ are complementary. A solution to either one determines a solution to both.

Linear programming problems are optimization problems in which the objective function and the constraints are all linear.

   a. Linear matrix inequality
   b. Topological derivative
   c. Linear programming relaxation
   d. Dual problem

18. In linear algebra, the _____ of a matrix A is another matrix $A^T$ created by any one of the following equivalent actions:

   - write the rows of A as the columns of $A^T$
   - write the columns of A as the rows of $A^T$
   - reflect A by its main diagonal to obtain $A^T$

Formally, the _____ of an m × n matrix A is the n × m matrix

$$A^T_{ij} = A_{ji} \text{ for } 1 \leq i \leq n, 1 \leq j \leq m.$$

- $\begin{bmatrix} 1 & 2 \\ 3 & 4 \end{bmatrix}^T = \begin{bmatrix} 1 & 3 \\ 2 & 4 \end{bmatrix}.$

- $\begin{bmatrix} 1 & 2 \\ 3 & 4 \\ 5 & 6 \end{bmatrix}^T = \begin{bmatrix} 1 & 3 & 5 \\ 2 & 4 & 6 \end{bmatrix}.$

For matrices A, B and scalar c we have the following properties of _____:

1. $\left(A^T\right)^T = A$

   Taking the _____ is an involution.

- $(A + B)^T = A^T + B^T$

## Chapter 6. Linear Programming: Simplex Method

The _____ respects addition.

- $(\mathbf{AB})^T = \mathbf{B}^T\mathbf{A}^T$

  Note that the order of the factors reverses. From this one can deduce that a square matrix A is invertible if and only if $A^T$ is invertible, and in this case we have $^T = ^{-1}$. It is relatively easy to extend this result to the general case of multiple matrices, where we find that $^T = Z^T Y^T X^T ... C^T B^T A^T$.

- $(c\mathbf{A})^T = c\mathbf{A}^T$

  The _____ of a scalar is the same scalar. Together with, this states that the _____ is a linear map from the space of m × n matrices to the space of all n × m matrices.

- $\det(\mathbf{A}^T) = \det(\mathbf{A})$

  The determinant of a matrix is the same as that of its _____.

- The dot product of two column vectors a and b can be computed as

  $$\mathbf{a} \cdot \mathbf{b} = \mathbf{a}^T \mathbf{b},$$

  which is written as $a_i b^i$ in Einstein notation.
- If A has only real entries, then $A^T A$ is a positive-semidefinite matrix.

- $(\mathbf{A}^T)^{-1} = (\mathbf{A}^{-1})^T$

  The _____ of an invertible matrix is also invertible, and its inverse is the _____ of the inverse of the original matrix.

- If A is a square matrix, then its eigenvalues are equal to the eigenvalues of its _____.

A square matrix whose _____ is equal to itself is called a symmetric matrix; that is, A is symmetric if

$$\mathbf{A}^T = \mathbf{A}.$$

A square matrix whose _____ is also its inverse is called an orthogonal matrix; that is, G is orthogonal if

$$\mathbf{G}\mathbf{G}^T = \mathbf{G}^T\mathbf{G} = \mathbf{I}_n, \text{ the identity matrix.}$$

70 Chapter 6. Linear Programming: Simplex Method

A square matrix whose _____ is equal to its negative is called skew-symmetric matrix; that is, A is skew-symmetric if

$$\mathbf{A}^{\mathrm{T}} = -\mathbf{A}.$$

The conjugate _____ of the complex matrix A, written as A*, is obtained by taking the _____ of A and the complex conjugate of each entry:

$$\mathbf{A}^{*} = (\overline{\mathbf{A}})^{\mathrm{T}} = \overline{(\mathbf{A}^{\mathrm{T}})}.$$

If f: V→W is a linear map between vector spaces V and W with nondegenerate bilinear forms, we define the _____ of f to be the linear map ${}^t f: W \rightarrow V$, determined by

$$B_V(v, {}^t f(w)) = B_W(f(v), w) \quad \forall \ v \in V, w \in W.$$

Here, $B_V$ and $B_W$ are the bilinear forms on V and W respectively. The matrix of the _____ of a map is the transposed matrix only if the bases are orthonormal with respect to their bilinear forms.

Over a complex vector space, one often works with sesquilinear forms instead of bilinear.

    a. Polynomial matrix
    b. Tridiagonal matrix
    c. Cartan matrix
    d. Transpose


19. In mathematics, a _____ is a rectangular table of elements, which may be numbers or, more generally, any abstract quantities that can be added and multiplied. Matrices are used to describe linear equations, keep track of the coefficients of linear transformations and to record data that depend on multiple parameters. Matrices are described by the field of _____ theory.
    a. Compression
    b. Coherent
    c. Double counting
    d. Matrix


20. In the geometry of the projective plane, _____ refers to geometric transformations that replace points by lines and lines by points while preserving incidence properties among the transformed objects. The existence of such transformations leads to a general principle, that any theorem about incidences between points and lines in the projective plane may be transformed into another theorem about lines and points, by a substitution of the appropriate words.

_____ in the projective plane is a special case of _____ for projective spaces, transformations that interchange

dimension + codimension.

a. Blocking
b. Decidable
c. Disk
d. Duality


21. In Linear programming a _____ is a variable which is subtracted from a constraint to turn the inequality into an equation.

This is required to turn an inequality into an equality where a linear combination of variables is greater than or equal to a given constant in the former. As with the other variables in the augmented constraints, the _____ cannot take on negative values, as the Simplex algorithm requires them to be positive or zero.

a. Global optimum
b. Quantum annealing
c. Successive linear programming
d. Surplus variable


22. _____ expresses an annual rate of interest taking into account the effect of compounding, usually for deposit or investment products. It is analogous to the Annual percentage rate, which is used for loans. In some jurisdictions, the use and definition of _____ may be regulated by a government agency, in which case it would generally be capitalized.

a. A chemical equation
b. A posteriori
c. A Mathematical Theory of Communication
d. Annual percentage yield


23. In mathematics, an _____, or central tendency of a data set refers to a measure of the 'middle' or 'expected' value of the data set. There are many different descriptive statistics that can be chosen as a measurement of the central tendency of the data items.

An _____ is a single value that is meant to typify a list of values.

a. A chemical equation
b. A posteriori
c. A Mathematical Theory of Communication
d. Average

24. In mathematics, a _____ is a way of expressing a number as a fraction of 100. It is often denoted using the percent sign, '%'. For example, 45% is equal to 45 / 100, or 0.45.
   a. Least common multiple
   b. Subtrahend
   c. Lowest common denominator
   d. Percentage

25. In mathematics, hyperbolic n-space, denoted $H^n$, is the maximally symmetric, simply connected, n-dimensional Riemannian manifold with constant sectional curvature −1. _____ is the principal example of a space exhibiting hyperbolic geometry. It can be thought of as the negative-curvature analogue of the n-sphere.
   a. Margulis lemma
   b. Hyperbolic geometry
   c. Horocycle
   d. Hyperbolic space

## Chapter 7. Logic, Sets, and Counting

1. _____ is the study of the principles of valid demonstration and inference. _____ is a branch of philosophy, a part of the classical trivium of grammar, _____, and rhetoric. of λογικïŒς, 'possessed of reason, intellectual, dialectical, argumentative', from λïŒγος logos, 'word, thought, idea, argument, account, reason, or principle'.
    a. Counterpart theory
    b. Satisfiability
    c. Boolean function
    d. Logic

2. In logic and mathematics, _____ or not is an operation on logical values, for example, the logical value of a proposition, that sends true to false and false to true. Intuitively, the _____ of a proposition holds exactly when that proposition does not hold. In grammar, nor is an adverb which acts as a coordinating conjunction.
    a. Syntax
    b. Sentence diagram
    c. 1-center problem
    d. Negation

3. In logic and philosophy, _____ refers to either (a) the 'content' or 'meaning' of a meaningful declarative sentence or (b) the pattern of symbols, marks, or sounds that make up a meaningful declarative sentence. _____s in either case are intended to be truth-bearers, that is, they are either true or false.

    The existence of _____s in the former sense, as well as the existence of 'meanings', is disputed.

    a. Linear logic
    b. Logicism
    c. Proposition
    d. Laws of classical logic

4. In logic and mathematics, or, also known as logical _____ or inclusive _____ is a logical operator that results in true whenever one or more of its operands are true. In grammar, or is a coordinating conjunction. In ordinary language 'or' rather has the meaning of exclusive _____.
    a. Disjunction
    b. Zero-point energy
    c. Cube
    d. Triquetra

5. In propositional logic, contraposition is a logical relationship between two statements of material implication. A proposition Q is materially implied by a proposition P when the following relationship holds:

$$(P \to Q)$$

In vernacular terms, this states 'If P then Q', or, 'If Socrates is a man then Socrates is human.' In a conditional such as this, P is called the antecedent and Q the consequent. One statement is the _____ of the other just when its antecedent is the negated consequent of the other, and vice-versa.

a. Contour map
b. Control chart
c. Continuous signal
d. Contrapositive

6. _____ is a concept in traditional logic referring to a 'type of immediate inference in which from a given proposition another proposition is inferred which has as its subject the predicate of the original proposition and as its predicate the subject of the original proposition (the quality of the proposition being retained).'

a. Boolean algebra
b. Foci
c. Field
d. Converse Logic

7. A _____ is a mathematical table used in logic -- specifically in connection with Boolean algebra, boolean functions, and propositional calculus -- to compute the functional values of logical expressions on each of their functional arguments, that is, on each combination of values taken by their logical variables. In particular, _____s can be used to tell whether a propositional expression is true for all legitimate input values, that is, logically valid.

The pattern of reasoning that the _____ tabulates was Frege's, Peirce's, and Schröder's by 1880.

a. 1-center problem
b. 120-cell
c. Truth table
d. 2-3 heap

8. In mathematics, _____ and undefined are used to explain whether or not expressions have meaningful, sensible, and unambiguous values. Not all branches of mathematics come to the same conclusion.

The following expressions are undefined in all contexts, but remarks in the analysis section may apply.

a. Defined
b. Plugging in
c. Toy model
d. LHS


9. In philosophy and logic, _____ is the status of facts that are not logically necessarily true or false.

In philosophy and logic, people draw a distinction between

- possibility: 'If it happened, it must be possible' -- If an event happened, it must be a possible event. A possible statement is not necessarily false. A 'possibility', such as a coincidence, is either a '_____', or a 'necessity' (but not both.)
- _____: a contingent event is an event which 'could have not happened'. Each contingent event is also a possible event, but not vice versa. A contingent statement is not necessarily false, but it is not necessarily true either.
- necessity: a necessary event is an event which 'could not have not happened'. In other words, a necessary event inevitably must have happened. Each necessary event is also a possible event, but not vice versa. A necessary statement is a statement that is necessarily true, such as a tautology.

a. Modal operator
b. Rigid designator
c. Modal companion
d. Contingency


10. In logic and mathematics, _____ is a logical relation that holds between a set T of formulae and a formula B when every model of T is also a model of B. In symbols,

1. $T \models B$
2. $T \Rightarrow B$
3. $T \therefore B$

which may be read 'T implies B, or 'B is a consequence of T'. In such an implication, T is called the antecedent, while B is called the consequent.

In other words, holds when the class of models of T is a subset of the class of models of B.

a. Necessary and sufficient
b. Logical implication
c. Thoralf Albert Skolem
d. Proposition

11. _____ In logic, statements p and q are logically equivalent if they have the same logical content.
a. Realizability
b. Distribution rule
c. Logical equivalence
d. Fallacies of definition

12. In mathematics, an _____ or member of a set is any one of the distinct objects that make up that set.

Writing A = {1,2,3,4}, means that the _____s of the set A are the numbers 1, 2, 3 and 4. Groups of _____s of A, for example {1,2}, are subsets of A.

a. Element
b. Order
c. Ideal
d. Universal code

13. In mathematics, and more specifically set theory, the _____ is the unique set having no members. Some axiomatic set theories assure that the _____ exists by including an axiom of _____; in other theories, its existence can be deduced. Many possible properties of sets are trivially true for the _____.
a. Inverse function
b. Empty function
c. A Mathematical Theory of Communication
d. Empty set

14. In mathematics, a _____ is a set that is negligible in some sense. For different applications, the meaning of 'negligible' varies. In measure theory, any set of measure 0 is called a _____.
a. Radonifying function
b. Borel-Cantelli lemma
c. Null set
d. Prevalence and shyness

## Chapter 7. Logic, Sets, and Counting

15. _____ is a branch of mathematics which focuses on the study of matrices. Initially a sub-branch of linear algebra, it has grown to cover subjects related to graph theory, algebra, combinatorics, and statistics as well.

The term matrix was first coined in 1848 by J.J. Sylvester as a name of an array of numbers.

   a. Matrix theory
   b. Segre classification
   c. Semi-simple operators
   d. Pairing

16. In mathematics, especially in set theory, a set A is a _____ of a set B if A is 'contained' inside B. Notice that A and B may coincide. The relationship of one set being a _____ of another is called inclusion.
   a. Horizontal line test
   b. Cartesian product
   c. Set of all sets
   d. Subset

17. In discrete mathematics and predominantly in set theory, a _____ is a concept used in comparisons of sets to refer to the unique values of one set in relation to another. The terms 'absolute' and 'relative' _____ refer to more specific applications of the concept, with universal _____s referring to elements unique to the universal set and the latter referring to the unique elements of one set in relation to another. In this image, the universal set is represented by the border of the image, and the set A as a disc.
   a. Kernel
   b. Derivative algebra
   c. Huge
   d. Complement

18. In mathematics, two sets are said to be disjoint if they have no element in common. For example, {1, 2, 3} and {4, 5, 6} are _____.

Formally, two sets A and B are disjoint if their intersection is the empty set.
wikimedia.org/math/b/3/5/b35d3befc06b831ff4d6cd63bf922efb.png">

This definition extends to any collection of sets.

a. Horizontal line test
b. Preimage
c. Disjoint sets
d. Subset



19. In mathematics, the _____ of two sets A and B is the set that contains all elements of A that also belong to B, but no other elements.

For explanation of the symbols used in this article, refer to the table of mathematical symbols.

The _____ of A and B

The _____ of A and B is written 'A ∩ B'. Formally:

> x is an element of A ∩ B if and only if
> - x is an element of A and
> - x is an element of B.
>
> For example:
> - The _____ of the sets {1, 2, 3} and {2, 3, 4} is {2, 3}.
> - The number 9 is not in the _____ of the set of prime numbers {2, 3, 5, 7, 11, â€¦} and the set of odd numbers {1, 3, 5, 7, 9, 11, â€¦}.

If the _____ of two sets A and B is empty, that is they have no elements in common, then they are said to be disjoint, denoted: A ∩ B = Ø. For example the sets {1, 2} and {3, 4} are disjoint, written {1, 2} ∩ {3, 4} = Ø.

a. Order
b. Intersection
c. Advice
d. Erlang



20. In set theory, the term _____ refers to a set operation used in the convergence of set elements to form a resultant set containing the elements of both sets. As a simple example, a _____ of two disjoint sets, which do not have elements in common results in a set containing all elements from both sets. A Venn diagram representing the _____ of sets A and B.
a. UES
b. Event
c. Introduction
d. Union

## Chapter 7. Logic, Sets, and Counting

21. _____ or set diagrams are diagrams that show all hypothetically possible logical relations between a finite collection of sets. _____ were invented around 1880 by John Venn. They are used in many fields, including set theory, probability, logic, statistics, and computer science.

   a. 120-cell
   b. 2-3 heap
   c. 1-center problem
   d. Venn diagrams


22. A _____ is a 2D geometric symbolic representation of information according to some visualization technique. Sometimes, the technique uses a 3D visualization which is then projected onto the 2D surface. The word graph is sometimes used as a synonym for _____.

   a. 120-cell
   b. 2-3 heap
   c. 1-center problem
   d. Diagram


23. In mathematics, hyperbolic n-space, denoted $H^n$, is the maximally symmetric, simply connected, n-dimensional Riemannian manifold with constant sectional curvature −1. _____ is the principal example of a space exhibiting hyperbolic geometry. It can be thought of as the negative-curvature analogue of the n-sphere.

   a. Margulis lemma
   b. Hyperbolic space
   c. Hyperbolic geometry
   d. Horocycle


24. _____ is the mathematical operation of scaling one number by another. It is one of the four basic operations in elementary arithmetic.

   _____ is defined for whole numbers in terms of repeated addition; for example, 4 multiplied by 3 can be calculated by adding 3 copies of 4 together:

   $$4 + 4 + 4 = 12.$$

   _____ of rational numbers and real numbers is defined by systematic generalization of this basic idea.

   a. Highest common factor
   b. Multiplication
   c. The number 0 is even.
   d. Least common multiple

25. In mathematics, a _____ is a statement that can be proved on the basis of explicitly stated or previously agreed assumptions.
   a. Theorem
   b. Disjunction introduction
   c. Boolean function
   d. Logical value

26. In mathematics, the _____ of a non-negative integer n, denoted by n!, is the product of all positive integers less than or equal to n. For example,

$$5! = 1 \times 2 \times 3 \times 4 \times 5 = 120$$

and
$$6! = 1 \times 2 \times 3 \times 4 \times 5 \times 6 = 720$$

The notation n! was introduced by Christian Kramp in 1808.

The _____ function is formally defined by

$$n! = \prod_{k=1}^{n} k \qquad \forall n \in \mathbb{N}.$$

The above definition incorporates the instance

$$0! = 1$$

as an instance of the fact that the product of no numbers at all is 1.

   a. Partition of a set
   b. Symbolic combinatorics
   c. Factorial
   d. Plane partition

27. _____ is usually defined as the activity of using and developing computer technology, computer hardware and software. It is the computer-specific part of information technology. Computer science (or _____ science) is the study and the science of the theoretical foundations of information and computation and their implementation and application in computer systems.

a. Deterministic finite state machine
b. Probabilistic Turing Machine
c. Computing
d. Parallel Random Access Machine

28. In several fields of mathematics the term _____ is used with different but closely related meanings. They all relate to the notion of mapping the elements of a set to other elements of the same set, i.e., exchanging elements of a set.

The general concept of _____ can be defined more formally in different contexts:

In combinatorics, a _____ is usually understood to be a sequence containing each element from a finite set once, and only once.

a. Tensor product
b. Permutation
c. Linearly independent
d. Cyclic permutation

29. In category theory, an abstract branch of mathematics, an _____ of a category C is an object I in C such that for every object X in C, there exists precisely one morphism I → X. The dual notion is that of a terminal object: T is terminal if for every object X in C there exists a single morphism X → T. _____s are also called coterminal, and terminal objects are also called final.

a. A chemical equation
b. A posteriori
c. Initial object
d. A Mathematical Theory of Communication

30. In computational complexity theory, an algorithm is said to take _____ if the asymptotic upper bound for the time it requires is proportional to the size of the input, which is usually denoted n.

Informally spoken, the running time increases linearly with the size of the input. For example, a procedure that adds up all elements of a list requires time proportional to the length of the list.

a. Linear time
b. Constructible function
c. Truth table reduction
d. Time-constructible function

## Chapter 7. Logic, Sets, and Counting

31. In combinatorial mathematics, a _____ is an un-ordered collection of distinct elements, usually of a prescribed size and taken from a given set. Given such a set S, a _____ of elements of S is just a subset of S, where as always forsets the order of the elements is not taken into account. Also, as always forsets, no elements can be repeated more than once in a _____; this is often referred to as a 'collection without repetition'.
   a. Sparsity
   b. Fill-in
   c. Heawood number
   d. Combination

32. A _____ is a software program that facilitates symbolic mathematics. The core functionality of a CAS is manipulation of mathematical expressions in symbolic form.

The symbolic manipulations supported typically include

- simplification to the smallest possible expression or some standard form, including automatic simplification with assumptions and simplification with constraints
- substitution of symbolic, functors or numeric values for expressions
- change of form of expressions: expanding products and powers, partial and full factorization, rewriting as partial fractions, constraint satisfaction, rewriting trigonometric functions as exponentials, etc.
- partial and total differentiation
- symbolic constrained and unconstrained global optimization
- solution of linear and some non-linear equations over various domains
- solution of some differential and difference equations
- taking some limits
- some indefinite and definite integration, including multidimensional integrals
- integral transforms
- arbitrary-precision numeric operations
- Series operations such as expansion, summation and products
- matrix operations including products, inverses, etc.
- display of mathematical expressions in two-dimensional mathematical form, often using typesetting systems similar to TeX
- add-ons for use in applied mathematics such as physics packages for physical computation
- plotting graphs and parametric plots of functions in two and three dimensions, and animating them
- APIs for linking it on an external program such as a database, or using in a programming language to use the _____
- drawing charts and diagrams
- string manipulation such as matching and searching
- statistical computation
- Theorem proving and verification
- graphic production and editing such as CGI and signal processing as image processing
- sound synthesis

Many also include a programming language, allowing users to implement their own algorithms.

Some _____s focus on a specific area of application; these are typically developed in academia and are free.

a. 2-3 heap
b. 120-cell
c. 1-center problem
d. Computer algebra system

## Chapter 8. Probability

1. _____ IPA: [pjɛʁ də fɛʁ'ma] (17 August 1601 or 1607/8 - 12 January 1665) was a French lawyer at the Parlement of Toulouse, France, and a mathematician who is given credit for early developments that led to modern calculus. In particular, he is recognized for his discovery of an original method of finding the greatest and the smallest ordinates of curved lines, which is analogous to that of the then unknown differential calculus, as well as his research into the theory of numbers. He also made notable contributions to analytic geometry, probability, and optics.

   a. Nikita Borisov
   b. Philip J. Davis
   c. Felix Hausdorff
   d. Pierre de Fermat


2. The word _____ denotes information gained by means of observation, experience as opposed to theoretical. A central concept in science and the scientific method is that all evidence must be _____ that is, dependent on evidence or consequences that are observable by the senses. It is usually differentiated from the philosophic usage of empiricism by the use of the adjective '_____' or the adverb 'empirically.' '_____' as an adjective or adverb is used in conjunction with both the natural and social sciences, and refers to the use of working hypotheses that are testable using observation or experiment.

   a. A chemical equation
   b. A posteriori
   c. A Mathematical Theory of Communication
   d. Empirical


3. _____ is the likelihood or chance that something is the case or will happen. Theoretical _____ is used extensively in areas such as statistics, mathematics, science and philosophy to draw conclusions about the likelihood of potential events and the underlying mechanics of complex systems.

   The word _____ does not have a consistent direct definition.

   a. Discrete random variable
   b. Standardized moment
   c. Probability
   d. Statistical significance


4. _____ is the branch of mathematics concerned with analysis of random phenomena. The central objects of _____ are random variables, stochastic processes, and events: mathematical abstractions of non-deterministic events or measured quantities that may either be single occurrences or evolve over time in an apparently random fashion. Although an individual coin toss or the roll of a die is a random event, if repeated many times the sequence of random events will exhibit certain statistical patterns, which can be studied and predicted.

*Chapter 8. Probability* 85

   a. Martingale central limit theorem
   b. Law of large numbers
   c. Standard probability space
   d. Probability theory

5. The word _____ has many distinct meanings in different fields of knowledge, depending on their methodologies and the context of discussion. Broadly speaking we can say that a _____ is some kind of belief or claim that (supposedly) explains, asserts, or consolidates some class of claims. Additionally, in contrast with a theorem the statement of the _____ is generally accepted only in some tentative fashion as opposed to regarding it as having been conclusively established.
   a. Theory
   b. Per mil
   c. Transport of structure
   d. Defined

6. In probability theory, an _____ is a set of outcomes to which a probability is assigned. Typically, when the sample space is finite, any subset of the sample space is an _____. However, this approach does not work well in cases where the sample space is infinite, most notably when the outcome is a real number.
   a. Equaliser
   b. Event
   c. Audio compression
   d. Information set

7. In scientific inquiry, an _____ is a method of investigating particular types of research questions or solving particular types of problems. The _____ is a cornerstone in the empirical approach to acquiring deeper knowledge about the world and is used in both natural sciences as well as in social sciences. An _____ is defined, in science, as a method of investigating less known fields, solving practical problems and proving theoretical assumptions.
   a. A chemical equation
   b. A posteriori
   c. A Mathematical Theory of Communication
   d. Experiment

8. In statistics, a _____ is a subset of a population. Typically, the population is very large, making a census or a complete enumeration of all the values in the population impractical or impossible. The _____ represents a subset of manageable size.

a. Duality
b. Sample
c. Boussinesq approximation
d. Dispersion

9. In probability theory, the _____ or universal _____, often denoted S, Ω of an experiment or random trial is the set of all possible outcomes. For example, if the experiment is tossing a coin, the _____ is the set {head, tail}. For tossing a single six-sided die, the _____ is {1, 2, 3, 4, 5, 6}.
   a. Sample space
   b. Markov chain
   c. Marginal distribution
   d. Martingale central limit theorem

10. In abstract algebra, a module S over a ring R is called _____ or irreducible if it is not the zero module 0 and if its only submodules are 0 and S. Understanding the _____ modules over a ring is usually helpful because these modules form the 'building blocks' of all other modules in a certain sense.

Abelian groups are the same as Z-modules.

   a. Basis
   b. Derivation
   c. Harmonic series
   d. Simple

11. In discrete mathematics and predominantly in set theory, a _____ is a concept used in comparisons of sets to refer to the unique values of one set in relation to another. The terms 'absolute' and 'relative' _____ refer to more specific applications of the concept, with universal _____s referring to elements unique to the universal set and the latter referring to the unique elements of one set in relation to another. In this image, the universal set is represented by the border of the image, and the set A as a disc.
   a. Kernel
   b. Derivative algebra
   c. Complement
   d. Huge

12. In mathematics, _____ and undefined are used to explain whether or not expressions have meaningful, sensible, and unambiguous values. Not all branches of mathematics come to the same conclusion.

The following expressions are undefined in all contexts, but remarks in the analysis section may apply.

a. Plugging in
b. LHS
c. Toy model
d. Defined

13. In game theory, an _____ is a set of moves or strategies taken by the players, or their payoffs resulting from the actions or strategies taken by all players. The two are complementary in that given knowledge of the set of strategies of all players, the final state of the game is known, as are any relevant payoffs. In a game where chance or a random event is involved, the _____ is not known from only the set of strategies, but is only realized when the random even are realized.
   a. Equaliser
   b. Outcome
   c. Autonomous system
   d. Algebraic

14. The mathematical concept of a _____ expresses the intuitive idea of deterministic dependence between two quantities, one of which is viewed as primary and the other as secondary. A _____ then is a way to associate a unique output for each input of a specified type, for example, a real number or an element of a given set.
   a. Going up
   b. Grill
   c. Coherent
   d. Function

15. _____ or experimental probability, is the ratio of the number favorable outcomes to the total number of trials , not in a sample space but in an actual sequence of experiments. In a more general sense, _____ estimates probabilities from experience and observation. The phrase a posteriori probability has also been used an alternative to _____ or relative frequency.
   a. A posteriori
   b. A chemical equation
   c. A Mathematical Theory of Communication
   d. Empirical probability

16. In statistics the _____ of an event i is the number $n_i$ of times the event occurred in the experiment or the study. These frequencies are often graphically represented in histograms.

We speak of absolute frequencies, when the counts $n_i$ themselves are given and of

$$f_i = \frac{n_i}{N} = \frac{n_i}{\sum_i n_i}$$

Taking the $f_i$ for all i and tabulating or plotting them leads to a _____ distribution.

a. Robinson-Dadson curves
b. Frequency
c. Digital room correction
d. Subharmonic

17. _____ is the interpretation of probability that defines an event's probability as the limit of its relative frequency in a large number of trials. The development of the frequentist account was motivated by the problems and paradoxes of the previously dominant viewpoint, the classical interpretation. The shift from the classical view to the frequentist view represents a paradigm shift in the progression of statistical thought.

a. 120-cell
b. Probabilistic proposition
c. Frequency Probability
d. 1-center problem

18. In mathematics, hyperbolic n-space, denoted $H^n$, is the maximally symmetric, simply connected, n-dimensional Riemannian manifold with constant sectional curvature −1. _____ is the principal example of a space exhibiting hyperbolic geometry. It can be thought of as the negative-curvature analogue of the n-sphere.

a. Hyperbolic geometry
b. Horocycle
c. Margulis lemma
d. Hyperbolic space

19. In mathematics, the _____ of two sets A and B is the set that contains all elements of A that also belong to B, but no other elements.

For explanation of the symbols used in this article, refer to the table of mathematical symbols.

The _____ of A and B

The _____ of A and B is written 'A ∩ B'. Formally:

> x is an element of A ∩ B if and only if
> - x is an element of A and
> - x is an element of B.
>
> For example:
> - The _____ of the sets {1, 2, 3} and {2, 3, 4} is {2, 3}.
> - The number 9 is not in the _____ of the set of prime numbers {2, 3, 5, 7, 11, â€¦} and the set of odd numbers {1, 3, 5, 7, 9, 11, â€¦}.

If the _____ of two sets A and B is empty, that is they have no elements in common, then they are said to be disjoint, denoted: A ∩ B = Ø. For example the sets {1, 2} and {3, 4} are disjoint, written
{1, 2} ∩ {3, 4} = Ø.

a. Order
b. Advice
c. Erlang
d. Intersection


20. In set theory, the term _____ refers to a set operation used in the convergence of set elements to form a resultant set containing the elements of both sets. As a simple example, a _____ of two disjoint sets, which do not have elements in common results in a set containing all elements from both sets. A Venn diagram representing the _____ of sets A and B.

a. UES
b. Event
c. Introduction
d. Union


21. In simple terms, two events are _____ if they cannot occur at the same time.

In logic, two _____ propositions are propositions that logically cannot both be true. To say that more than two propositions are _____ may, depending on context mean that no two of them can both be true, or only that they cannot all be true.

a. Mutually exclusive
b. Philosophy of mathematics
c. Philosophy
d. Determinism

22. In probability theory and statistics the _____ in favour of an event or a proposition are the quantity p /, where p is the probability of the event or proposition. The _____ against the same event are / p. For example, if you chose a random day of the week, then the _____ that you would choose a Sunday would be 1/6, not 1/7.
   a. Event
   b. Anscombe transform
   c. Estimation of covariance matrices
   d. Odds


23. A _____ is a structured activity, usually undertaken for enjoyment and sometimes also used as an educational tool. _____s are distinct from work, which is usually carried out for remuneration, and from art, which is more concerned with the expression of ideas. However, the distinction is not clear-cut, and many _____s are also considered to be work (such as professional players of spectator sports/_____s) or art (such as jigsaw puzzles or _____s involving an artistic layout such as Mah-jongg solitaire.)
   a. Game
   b. 120-cell
   c. 2-3 heap
   d. 1-center problem


24. The _____ is a theorem in probability that describes the long-term stability of the mean of a random variable. Given a random variable with a finite expected value, if its values are repeatedly sampled, as the number of these observations increases, their mean will tend to approach and stay close to the expected value.

The LLN can easily be illustrated using the rolls of a die.

   a. Graphical model
   b. Law of large numbers
   c. Point process
   d. Random field


25. A _____ is a software program that facilitates symbolic mathematics. The core functionality of a CAS is manipulation of mathematical expressions in symbolic form.

The symbolic manipulations supported typically include

- simplification to the smallest possible expression or some standard form, including automatic simplification with assumptions and simplification with constraints
- substitution of symbolic, functors or numeric values for expressions
- change of form of expressions: expanding products and powers, partial and full factorization, rewriting as partial fractions, constraint satisfaction, rewriting trigonometric functions as exponentials, etc.
- partial and total differentiation
- symbolic constrained and unconstrained global optimization
- solution of linear and some non-linear equations over various domains
- solution of some differential and difference equations
- taking some limits
- some indefinite and definite integration, including multidimensional integrals
- integral transforms
- arbitrary-precision numeric operations
- Series operations such as expansion, summation and products
- matrix operations including products, inverses, etc.
- display of mathematical expressions in two-dimensional mathematical form, often using typesetting systems similar to TeX
- add-ons for use in applied mathematics such as physics packages for physical computation
- plotting graphs and parametric plots of functions in two and three dimensions, and animating them
- APIs for linking it on an external program such as a database, or using in a programming language to use the _____
- drawing charts and diagrams
- string manipulation such as matching and searching
- statistical computation
- Theorem proving and verification
- graphic production and editing such as CGI and signal processing as image processing
- sound synthesis

Many also include a programming language, allowing users to implement their own algorithms.

Some _____s focus on a specific area of application; these are typically developed in academia and are free.

a. 1-center problem
b. 120-cell
c. 2-3 heap
d. Computer algebra system

## Chapter 8. Probability

26. In mathematics and physics, there are a _____ number of topics named in honor of Leonhard Euler. As well, many of these topics include their own unique function, equation, formula, identity, number, or other mathematical entity. Unfortunately however, many of these entities have been given simple names like Euler's function, Euler's equation, and Euler's formula, which are further confused by variations of the 'Euler'-prefix Overall though, Euler's work touched upon so many fields that he is often the earliest written reference on a given matter.
   a. List of trigonometry topics
   b. List of integrals of logarithmic functions
   c. List of mathematical knots and links
   d. Large

27. _____ is the probability of some event A, given the occurrence of some other event B. _____ is written P[A│B], and is read 'the probability of A, given B'.

Joint probability is the probability of two events in conjunction. That is, it is the probability of both events together. The joint probability of A and B is written $P(A \cap B)$ or $P(A,B)$.

   a. Renewal theory
   b. Quantile
   c. Sample space
   d. Conditional probability

28. The _____ governs the differentiation of products of differentiable functions.
   a. 1-center problem
   b. Product rule
   c. 120-cell
   d. Reciprocal Rule

29. In mathematics, a _____ is a statement that can be proved on the basis of explicitly stated or previously agreed assumptions.
   a. Theorem
   b. Boolean function
   c. Disjunction introduction
   d. Logical value

30. In set theory, a _____ is a partially ordered set such that for each t ∈ T, the set {s ∈ T : s < t} is well-ordered by the relation <. For each t ∈ T, the order type of {s ∈ T : s < t} is called the height of t. The height of T itself is the least ordinal greater than the height of each element of T.

## Chapter 8. Probability

a. Transitive reduction
b. Set-theoretic topology
c. Tree
d. Definable numbers

31. A _____ is the counterpart to a deterministic process in probability theory. Instead of dealing with only one possible 'reality' of how the process might evolve under time, in a stochastic or random process there is some indeterminacy in its future evolution described by probability distributions. This means that even if the initial condition is known, there are many possibilities the process might go to, but some paths are more probable and others less.

   a. Fractional Brownian motion
   b. Mixing time
   c. Stochastic simulation
   d. Stochastic process

32. In graph theory, an _____ or stable set is a set of vertices in a graph no two of which are adjacent. That is, it is a set V of vertices such that for every two vertices in V, there is no edge connecting the two. Equivalently, each edge in the graph has at most one endpoint in V.

   a. Instant Insanity
   b. Isomorphism of graphs
   c. Eulerian path
   d. Independent set

33. In mathematics and in the sciences, a _____ (plural: _____e, formulæ or _____s) is a concise way of expressing information symbolically (as in a mathematical or chemical _____), or a general relationship between quantities. One of many famous _____e is Albert Einstein's E = mc² (see special relativity

In mathematics, a _____ is a key to solve an equation with variables. For example, the problem of determining the volume of a sphere is one that requires a significant amount of integral calculus to solve.

   a. 120-cell
   b. 2-3 heap
   c. 1-center problem
   d. Formula

34. In probability theory and statistics, a _____ identifies either the probability of each value of an unidentified random variable, or the probability of the value falling within a particular interval. The probability function describes the range of possible values that a random variable can attain and the probability that the value of the random variable is within any subset of that range.

When the random variable takes values in the set of real numbers, the _____ is completely described by the cumulative distribution function, whose value at each real x is the probability that the random variable is smaller than or equal to x.

   a. Normal distribution
   b. Z-test
   c. Statistical graphics
   d. Probability distribution

35. In mathematics, _____ are used in the study of chance and probability. They were developed to assist in the analysis of games of chance, stochastic events, and the results of scientific experiments by capturing only the mathematical properties necessary to answer probabilistic questions. Further formalizations have firmly grounded the entity in the theoretical domains of mathematics by making use of measure theory.
   a. Statistics
   b. Random variables
   c. Median polish
   d. Statistical dispersion

36. In differential geometry, a discipline within mathematics, a _____ is a subset of the tangent bundle of a manifold satisfying certain properties. _____s are used to build up notions of integrability, and specifically of a foliation of a manifold
   a. Coherence
   b. Constraint
   c. Discontinuity
   d. Distribution

37. In probability theory and statistics, the _____ of a random variable is the integral of the random variable with respect to its probability measure. For discrete random variables this is equivalent to the probability-weighted sum of the possible values, and for continuous random variables with a density function it is the probability density -weighted integral of the possible values.

The _____ may be intuitively understood by the law of large numbers: The _____, when it exists, is almost surely the limit of the sample mean as sample size grows to infinity.

a. Infinitely divisible distribution
b. Expected value
c. Illustration
d. Event



38. In statistics, a _____ is a graphical display of tabulated frequencies, shown as bars. It shows what proportion of cases fall into each of several categories. A _____ differs from a bar chart in that it is the area of the bar that denotes the value, not the height as in bar charts, a crucial distinction when the categories are not of uniform width.
   a. Probability distribution
   b. Standardized moment
   c. First-hitting-time models
   d. Histogram



39. _____ can be regarded as an outcome of mental processes leading to the selection of a course of action among several alternatives. Every _____ process produces a final choice. The output can be an action or an opinion of choice.
   a. 2-3 heap
   b. 120-cell
   c. 1-center problem
   d. Decision making

# Chapter 9. Markov Chains

1. In mathematics, a _____, named after Andrey Markov, is a stochastic process with the Markov property. Having the Markov property means that, given the present state, future states are independent of the past states. In other words, the description of the present state fully captures all the information that could influence the future evolution of the process. Future states will be reached through a probabilistic process instead of a deterministic one.
   a. Law of Truly Large Numbers
   b. Variance-to-mean ratio
   c. Markov chain
   d. Possibility theory

2. A _____ is the counterpart to a deterministic process in probability theory. Instead of dealing with only one possible 'reality' of how the process might evolve under time, in a stochastic or random process there is some indeterminacy in its future evolution described by probability distributions. This means that even if the initial condition is known, there are many possibilities the process might go to, but some paths are more probable and others less.
   a. Fractional Brownian motion
   b. Mixing time
   c. Stochastic simulation
   d. Stochastic process

3. A _____ is a 2D geometric symbolic representation of information according to some visualization technique. Sometimes, the technique uses a 3D visualization which is then projected onto the 2D surface. The word graph is sometimes used as a synonym for _____.
   a. 2-3 heap
   b. 120-cell
   c. 1-center problem
   d. Diagram

4. In mathematics, a _____ is a rectangular table of elements, which may be numbers or, more generally, any abstract quantities that can be added and multiplied. Matrices are used to describe linear equations, keep track of the coefficients of linear transformations and to record data that depend on multiple parameters. Matrices are described by the field of _____ theory.
   a. Matrix
   b. Coherent
   c. Double counting
   d. Compression

5. _____ is the likelihood or chance that something is the case or will happen. Theoretical _____ is used extensively in areas such as statistics, mathematics, science and philosophy to draw conclusions about the likelihood of potential events and the underlying mechanics of complex systems.

## Chapter 9. Markov Chains

The word _____ does not have a consistent direct definition.

a. Standardized moment
b. Probability
c. Discrete random variable
d. Statistical significance

6. In differential geometry, a discipline within mathematics, a _____ is a subset of the tangent bundle of a manifold satisfying certain properties. _____s are used to build up notions of integrability, and specifically of a foliation of a manifold

a. Distribution
b. Constraint
c. Discontinuity
d. Coherence

7. In mathematics, a stochastic matrix, probability matrix, or _____ is used to describe the transitions of a Markov chain. It has found use in probability theory, statistics and linear algebra, as well as computer science. There are several different definitions and types of stochastic matrices;

    A right stochastic matrix is a square matrix each of whose rows consists of nonnegative real numbers, with each row summing to 1.

a. Sylvester matrix
b. Hessenberg matrix
c. Pick matrix
d. Transition matrix

8. In mathematics, _____ and undefined are used to explain whether or not expressions have meaningful, sensible, and unambiguous values. Not all branches of mathematics come to the same conclusion.

The following expressions are undefined in all contexts, but remarks in the analysis section may apply.

a. Plugging in
b. Defined
c. LHS
d. Toy model

9. In mathematics, hyperbolic n-space, denoted $H^n$, is the maximally symmetric, simply connected, n-dimensional Riemannian manifold with constant sectional curvature −1. _____ is the principal example of a space exhibiting hyperbolic geometry. It can be thought of as the negative-curvature analogue of the n-sphere.

   a. Hyperbolic geometry
   b. Horocycle
   c. Margulis lemma
   d. Hyperbolic space

10. _____ is a branch of mathematics which focuses on the study of matrices. Initially a sub-branch of linear algebra, it has grown to cover subjects related to graph theory, algebra, combinatorics, and statistics as well.

The term matrix was first coined in 1848 by J.J. Sylvester as a name of an array of numbers.

   a. Segre classification
   b. Matrix theory
   c. Semi-simple operators
   d. Pairing

11. _____ Any process by which a specified characteristic usually amplitude of the output of a device is prevented from exceeding a predetermined value.

   a. Parametric continuity
   b. Notation
   c. Logical equivalence
   d. Limiting

12. A _____ is a software program that facilitates symbolic mathematics. The core functionality of a CAS is manipulation of mathematical expressions in symbolic form.

## Chapter 9. Markov Chains

The symbolic manipulations supported typically include

- simplification to the smallest possible expression or some standard form, including automatic simplification with assumptions and simplification with constraints
- substitution of symbolic, functors or numeric values for expressions
- change of form of expressions: expanding products and powers, partial and full factorization, rewriting as partial fractions, constraint satisfaction, rewriting trigonometric functions as exponentials, etc.
- partial and total differentiation
- symbolic constrained and unconstrained global optimization
- solution of linear and some non-linear equations over various domains
- solution of some differential and difference equations
- taking some limits
- some indefinite and definite integration, including multidimensional integrals
- integral transforms
- arbitrary-precision numeric operations
- Series operations such as expansion, summation and products
- matrix operations including products, inverses, etc.
- display of mathematical expressions in two-dimensional mathematical form, often using typesetting systems similar to TeX
- add-ons for use in applied mathematics such as physics packages for physical computation
- plotting graphs and parametric plots of functions in two and three dimensions, and animating them
- APIs for linking it on an external program such as a database, or using in a programming language to use the _____
- drawing charts and diagrams
- string manipulation such as matching and searching
- statistical computation
- Theorem proving and verification
- graphic production and editing such as CGI and signal processing as image processing
- sound synthesis

Many also include a programming language, allowing users to implement their own algorithms.

Some _____s focus on a specific area of application; these are typically developed in academia and are free.

a. 2-3 heap
b. 120-cell
c. Computer algebra system
d. 1-center problem

13. A _____ is a device for performing mathematical calculations, distinguished from a computer by having a limited problem solving ability and an interface optimized for interactive calculation rather than programming. _____s can be hardware or software, and mechanical or electronic, and are often built into devices such as PDAs or mobile phones.

Modern electronic _____s are generally small, digital, and usually inexpensive.

   a. 2-3 heap
   b. 120-cell
   c. 1-center problem
   d. Calculator

14. A _____ typically refers to a class of handheld calculators that are capable of plotting graphs, solving simultaneous equations, and performing numerous other tasks with variables. Most popular _____s are also programmable, allowing the user to create customized programs, typically for scientific/engineering and education applications. Due to their large displays intended for graphing, they can also accommodate several lines of text and calculations at a time.
   a. Genus
   b. Graphing calculator
   c. Bump mapping
   d. Support vector machines

15. In simple terms, two events are _____ if they cannot occur at the same time.

In logic, two _____ propositions are propositions that logically cannot both be true. To say that more than two propositions are _____ may, depending on context mean that no two of them can both be true, or only that they cannot all be true.

   a. Determinism
   b. Philosophy of mathematics
   c. Philosophy
   d. Mutually exclusive

16. In probability theory, an _____ is a set of outcomes to which a probability is assigned. Typically, when the sample space is finite, any subset of the sample space is an _____. However, this approach does not work well in cases where the sample space is infinite, most notably when the outcome is a real number.

a. Equaliser
b. Audio compression
c. Information set
d. Event

17. _____, also sometimes known as standard form or as exponential notation, is a way of writing numbers that accommodates values too large or small to be conveniently written in standard decimal notation. _____ has a number of useful properties and is often favored by scientists, mathematicians and engineers, who work with such numbers.

In _____, numbers are written in the form:

$$a \times 10^b$$

a. Leading zero
b. 1-center problem
c. Radix point
d. Scientific notation

18. In classical differential geometry, _____ refers to the simple idea of rolling one smooth surface over another in Euclidean space. For example, the tangent plane to a surface at a point can be rolled around the surface to obtain the tangent-plane at other points.

The tangential contact between the surfaces being rolled over one another provides a relation between points on the two surfaces.

a. FISH
b. Double counting
c. Development
d. Blinding

19. _____ is a legal term (in some jurisdictions, notably in the USA, United Kingdom, Canada, and Australia) that encompasses land along with anything permanently affixed to the land, such as buildings, specifically property that is stationary, or fixed in location. _____ law is the body of regulations and legal codes which pertain to such matters under a particular jurisdiction. _____ is often considered synonymous with real property (also sometimes called realty), in contrast with personal property (also sometimes called chattel or personalty under chattel law or personal property law.)

a. 1-center problem
b. Home equity
c. 120-cell
d. Real estate

20. In mathematics, a _____ is a statement that can be proved on the basis of explicitly stated or previously agreed assumptions.
a. Disjunction introduction
b. Logical value
c. Boolean function
d. Theorem

## Chapter 10. Games and Decisions

1. _____s is the social science that studies the production, distribution, and consumption of goods and services.

The term _____s comes from the Ancient Greek οἰκονομία (oikonomia, 'management of a household, administration') from οἶκος (oikos, 'house') + νόμος (nomos, 'custom' or 'law'), hence 'rules of the house(hold)'.

Current _____ models developed out of the broader field of political economy in the late 19$^{th}$ century, owing to a desire to use an empirical approach more akin to the physical sciences.

   a. A Mathematical Theory of Communication
   b. Experimental economics
   c. A chemical equation
   d. Economic


2. A _____ is a structured activity, usually undertaken for enjoyment and sometimes also used as an educational tool. _____s are distinct from work, which is usually carried out for remuneration, and from art, which is more concerned with the expression of ideas. However, the distinction is not clear-cut, and many _____s are also considered to be work (such as professional players of spectator sports/_____s) or art (such as jigsaw puzzles or _____s involving an artistic layout such as Mah-jongg solitaire.)
   a. 120-cell
   b. 1-center problem
   c. 2-3 heap
   d. Game


3. _____ is a branch of applied mathematics that is used in the social sciences, biology, engineering, political science, international relations, computer science, and philosophy. _____ attempts to mathematically capture behavior in strategic situations, in which an individual's success in making choices depends on the choices of others. While initially developed to analyze competitions in which one individual does better at another's expense, it has been expanded to treat a wide class of interactions, which are classified according to several criteria.
   a. Game theory
   b. Mathematical economics
   c. Consumer theory
   d. Computational economic


4. _____ is a journal of game theory published by Elsevier. First published in 1989, it is considered to be the leading journal of game theory and one of the top journals in economics. It is one of the two official journals of the Game Theory Society.

*Chapter 10. Games and Decisions*

a. 120-cell
b. 2-3 heap
c. 1-center problem
d. Games and Economic Behavior

5. _____ was a Hungarian American mathematician who made major contributions to a vast range of fields, including set theory, functional analysis, quantum mechanics, ergodic theory, continuous geometry, economics and game theory, computer science, numerical analysis, hydrodynamics, and statistics, as well as many other mathematical fields. He is generally regarded as one of the foremost mathematicians of the 20th century. The mathematician Jean Dieudonné called von Neumann 'the last of the great mathematicians.' Most notably, von Neumann was a pioneer of the application of operator theory to quantum mechanics, a principal member of the Manhattan Project and the Institute for Advanced Study in Princeton, and a key figure in the development of game theory and the concepts of cellular automata and the universal constructor.
   a. Stuart Milner-Barry
   b. John von Neumann
   c. Hemachandra SurÄ«
   d. Frederick William Winterbotham

6. The word _____ has many distinct meanings in different fields of knowledge, depending on their methodologies and the context of discussion. Broadly speaking we can say that a _____ is some kind of belief or claim that (supposedly) explains, asserts, or consolidates some class of claims. Additionally, in contrast with a theorem the statement of the _____ is generally accepted only in some tentative fashion as opposed to regarding it as having been conclusively established.
   a. Per mil
   b. Transport of structure
   c. Defined
   d. Theory

7. In mathematics, a _____ is a rectangular table of elements, which may be numbers or, more generally, any abstract quantities that can be added and multiplied. Matrices are used to describe linear equations, keep track of the coefficients of linear transformations and to record data that depend on multiple parameters. Matrices are described by the field of _____ theory.
   a. Compression
   b. Double counting
   c. Coherent
   d. Matrix

8. A _____, in mathematics, is a polynomial function of the form $f(x) = ax^2 + bx + c$, where $a \neq 0$. The graph of a _____ is a parabola whose major axis is parallel to the y-axis.

## Chapter 10. Games and Decisions

The expression $ax^2 + bx + c$ in the definition of a _____ is a polynomial of degree 2 or a 2nd degree polynomial, because the highest exponent of x is 2.

   a. Multivariate division algorithm
   b. Quadratic function
   c. Laguerre polynomials
   d. Discriminant


9. In mathematics, _____ and undefined are used to explain whether or not expressions have meaningful, sensible, and unambiguous values. Not all branches of mathematics come to the same conclusion.

The following expressions are undefined in all contexts, but remarks in the analysis section may apply.

   a. Toy model
   b. Plugging in
   c. LHS
   d. Defined


10. The mathematical concept of a _____ expresses the intuitive idea of deterministic dependence between two quantities, one of which is viewed as primary and the other as secondary. A _____ then is a way to associate a unique output for each input of a specified type, for example, a real number or an element of a given set.
   a. Grill
   b. Coherent
   c. Function
   d. Going up


11. In game theory, a player's _____ in a game is a complete plan of action for whatever situation might arise; this fully determines the player's behaviour. A player's _____ will determine the action the player will take at any stage of the game, for every possible history of play up to that stage.

A _____ profile is a set of strategies for each player which fully specifies all actions in a game.

   a. Strategy
   b. Sir Philip Sidney game
   c. Correlated equilibrium
   d. Matching pennies

12. In probability theory and statistics, the _____ of a random variable is the integral of the random variable with respect to its probability measure. For discrete random variables this is equivalent to the probability-weighted sum of the possible values, and for continuous random variables with a density function it is the probability density -weighted integral of the possible values.

The _____ may be intuitively understood by the law of large numbers: The _____, when it exists, is almost surely the limit of the sample mean as sample size grows to infinity.

   a. Event
   b. Expected value
   c. Infinitely divisible distribution
   d. Illustration

13. In mathematics, a _____ is a statement that can be proved on the basis of explicitly stated or previously agreed assumptions.
   a. Logical value
   b. Boolean function
   c. Disjunction introduction
   d. Theorem

14. In mathematics, _____ is a technique for optimization of a linear objective function, subject to linear equality and linear inequality constraints. Informally, _____ determines the way to achieve the best outcome in a given mathematical model given some list of requirements represented as linear equations.

More formally, given a polytope, and a real-valued affine function

$$f(x_1, x_2, \ldots, x_n) = c_1 x_1 + c_2 x_2 + \cdots + c_n x_n + d$$

defined on this polytope, a _____ method will find a point in the polytope where this function has the smallest value.

   a. Lin-Kernighan
   b. Linear programming relaxation
   c. Descent direction
   d. Linear programming

15. A _____ is a software program that facilitates symbolic mathematics. The core functionality of a CAS is manipulation of mathematical expressions in symbolic form.

## Chapter 10. Games and Decisions

The symbolic manipulations supported typically include

- simplification to the smallest possible expression or some standard form, including automatic simplification with assumptions and simplification with constraints
- substitution of symbolic, functors or numeric values for expressions
- change of form of expressions: expanding products and powers, partial and full factorization, rewriting as partial fractions, constraint satisfaction, rewriting trigonometric functions as exponentials, etc.
- partial and total differentiation
- symbolic constrained and unconstrained global optimization
- solution of linear and some non-linear equations over various domains
- solution of some differential and difference equations
- taking some limits
- some indefinite and definite integration, including multidimensional integrals
- integral transforms
- arbitrary-precision numeric operations
- Series operations such as expansion, summation and products
- matrix operations including products, inverses, etc.
- display of mathematical expressions in two-dimensional mathematical form, often using typesetting systems similar to TeX
- add-ons for use in applied mathematics such as physics packages for physical computation
- plotting graphs and parametric plots of functions in two and three dimensions, and animating them
- APIs for linking it on an external program such as a database, or using in a programming language to use the _____
- drawing charts and diagrams
- string manipulation such as matching and searching
- statistical computation
- Theorem proving and verification
- graphic production and editing such as CGI and signal processing as image processing
- sound synthesis

Many also include a programming language, allowing users to implement their own algorithms.

Some _____s focus on a specific area of application; these are typically developed in academia and are free.

a. 120-cell
b. 1-center problem
c. 2-3 heap
d. Computer algebra system

16. In the mathematical area of order theory, every partially ordered set P gives rise to a _____ partially ordered set which is often denoted by P$^{op}$ or P$^d$. This _____ order P$^{op}$ is defined to be the set with the inverse order. It is easy to see that this construction, which can be depicted by flipping the Hasse diagram for P upside down, will indeed yield a partially ordered set.

   a. Dual
   b. Christofides heuristics
   c. Context-sensitive language
   d. Contraction mapping



17. In linear programming, the primary problem and the _____ are complementary. A solution to either one determines a solution to both.

Linear programming problems are optimization problems in which the objective function and the constraints are all linear.

   a. Dual problem
   b. Linear matrix inequality
   c. Topological derivative
   d. Linear programming relaxation



18. In geometry, a _____ or n-_____ is an n-dimensional analogue of a triangle. Specifically, a _____ is the convex hull of a set of affinely independent points in some Euclidean space of dimension n or higher.

For example, a 0-_____ is a point, a 1-_____ is a line segment, a 2-_____ is a triangle, a 3-_____ is a tetrahedron, and a 4-_____ is a pentachoron.

   a. Polytetrahedron
   b. Hypercell
   c. Demihypercubes
   d. Simplex



19. In mathematical optimization theory, the simplex algorithm, created by the American mathematician George Dantzig in 1947, is a popular algorithm for numerical solution of the linear programming problem. The journal Computing in Science and Engineering listed it as one of the top 10 algorithms of the century.

An unrelated, but similarly named method is the Nelder-Mead method or downhill _____ due to Nelder ' Mead and is a numerical method for optimising many-dimensional unconstrained problems, belonging to the more general class of search algorithms.

a. Fibonacci search
b. Hill climbing
c. Differential evolution
d. Simplex method

20. In mathematics, hyperbolic n-space, denoted $H^n$, is the maximally symmetric, simply connected, n-dimensional Riemannian manifold with constant sectional curvature −1. _____ is the principal example of a space exhibiting hyperbolic geometry. It can be thought of as the negative-curvature analogue of the n-sphere.
   a. Margulis lemma
   b. Horocycle
   c. Hyperbolic geometry
   d. Hyperbolic space

# Chapter 11. Data Description and Probability Distributions

1. A bar chart or _____ is a chart with rectangular bars with lengths proportional to the values that they represent. Bar charts are used for comparing two or more values. The bars can be horizontally or vertically oriented.
   a. 1-center problem
   b. 2-3 heap
   c. Bar graph
   d. 120-cell

2. _____: A graph using line segments to join the plotted points to represent data over time.
   a. Closed under some operation
   b. Conditional factor demand
   c. Control theory
   d. Broken-line graph

3. In set theory and its applications throughout mathematics, a _____ is a collection of sets that can be unambiguously defined by a property that all its members share. The precise definition of '_____' depends on foundational context. In work on ZF set theory, the notion of _____ is informal, whereas other set theories, such as NBG set theory, axiomatize the notion of '_____'.
   a. Class
   b. Congruent
   c. Coherence
   d. Filter

4. In statistics the _____ of an event i is the number $n_i$ of times the event occurred in the experiment or the study. These frequencies are often graphically represented in histograms.

   We speak of absolute frequencies, when the counts $n_i$ themselves are given and of

   $$f_i = \frac{n_i}{N} = \frac{n_i}{\sum_i n_i}$$

   Taking the $f_i$ for all i and tabulating or plotting them leads to a _____ distribution.

   a. Robinson-Dadson curves
   b. Digital room correction
   c. Subharmonic
   d. Frequency

## Chapter 11. Data Description and Probability Distributions

5. In statistics, a _____ is a list of the values that a variable takes in a sample. It is usually a list, ordered by quantity, showing the number of times each value appears. For example, if 100 people rate a five-point Likert scale assessing their agreement with a statement on a scale on which 1 denotes strong agreement and 5 strong disagreement, the _____ of their responses might look like:

This simple tabulation has two drawbacks.

   a. Covariance
   b. Percentile
   c. Confounding
   d. Frequency distribution

6. In differential geometry, a discipline within mathematics, a _____ is a subset of the tangent bundle of a manifold satisfying certain properties. _____s are used to build up notions of integrability, and specifically of a foliation of a manifold
   a. Distribution
   b. Discontinuity
   c. Constraint
   d. Coherence

7. The _____ or Dirac's delta is a mathematical construct introduced by the British theoretical physicist Paul Dirac. Informally, it is a function representing an infinitely sharp peak bounding unit area: a function that has the value zero everywhere except at x = 0 where its value is infinitely large in such a way that its total integral is 1. It is a continuous analogue of the discrete Kronecker delta.
   a. Hyperfunction
   b. Weak derivative
   c. Dirac delta
   d. Schwartz kernel theorem

8. In mathematics, a _____ is a set of real numbers with the property that any number that lies between two numbers in the set is also included in the set. For example, the set of all numbers x satisfying $0 \leq x \leq 1$ is an _____ which contains 0 and 1, as well as all numbers between them. Other examples of _____s are the set of all real numbers $\mathbb{R}$, the set of all positive real numbers, and the empty set.
   a. Order
   b. Annihilator
   c. Ideal
   d. Interval

9. In descriptive statistics, the _____ is the length of the smallest interval which contains all the data. It is calculated by subtracting the smallest observations from the greatest and provides an indication of statistical dispersion.

It is measured in the same units as the data.

   a. Kernel
   b. Class
   c. Range
   d. Bandwidth


10. _____ is the likelihood or chance that something is the case or will happen. Theoretical _____ is used extensively in areas such as statistics, mathematics, science and philosophy to draw conclusions about the likelihood of potential events and the underlying mechanics of complex systems.

The word _____ does not have a consistent direct definition.

   a. Discrete random variable
   b. Probability
   c. Statistical significance
   d. Standardized moment


11. In probability theory and statistics, a _____ identifies either the probability of each value of an unidentified random variable, or the probability of the value falling within a particular interval. The probability function describes the range of possible values that a random variable can attain and the probability that the value of the random variable is within any subset of that range.

When the random variable takes values in the set of real numbers, the _____ is completely described by the cumulative distribution function, whose value at each real x is the probability that the random variable is smaller than or equal to x.

   a. Probability distribution
   b. Statistical graphics
   c. Normal distribution
   d. Z-test


12. A _____ is the result of applying a function to a set of data.

## Chapter 11. Data Description and Probability Distributions

More formally, statistical theory defines a _____ as a function of a sample where the function itself is independent of the sample's distribution: the term is used both for the function and for the value of the function on a given sample.

A _____ is distinct from an unknown statistical parameter, which is not computable from a sample.

  a. Statistic
  b. Spatial dependence
  c. Parameter space
  d. Loss function


13. _____ is a mathematical science pertaining to the collection, analysis, interpretation or explanation, and presentation of data. It also provides tools for prediction and forecasting based on data. It is applicable to a wide variety of academic disciplines, from the natural and social sciences to the humanities, government and business.
  a. Regression toward the mean
  b. Probability distribution
  c. Percentile rank
  d. Statistics


14. In mathematics, _____ and undefined are used to explain whether or not expressions have meaningful, sensible, and unambiguous values. Not all branches of mathematics come to the same conclusion.

The following expressions are undefined in all contexts, but remarks in the analysis section may apply.

  a. Toy model
  b. Defined
  c. LHS
  d. Plugging in


15. In statistics, a _____ is a graphical display of tabulated frequencies, shown as bars. It shows what proportion of cases fall into each of several categories. A _____ differs from a bar chart in that it is the area of the bar that denotes the value, not the height as in bar charts, a crucial distinction when the categories are not of uniform width.
  a. Probability distribution
  b. First-hitting-time models
  c. Standardized moment
  d. Histogram

16. In mathematics, the concept of a _____ tries to capture the intuitive idea of a geometrical one-dimensional and continuous object. A simple example is the circle. In everyday use of the term '_____', a straight line is not curved, but in mathematical parlance _____s include straight lines and line segments.
    a. Curve
    b. Quadrifolium
    c. Kappa curve
    d. Negative pedal curve

17. In geometry a _____ is traditionally a plane figure that is bounded by a closed path or circuit, composed of a finite sequence of straight line segments. These segments are called its edges or sides, and the points where two edges meet are the _____'s vertices or corners. The interior of the _____ is sometimes called its body.
    a. Polygonal curve
    b. Regular polygon
    c. Parallelogon
    d. Polygon

18. _____ are used in computer graphics to compose images that are three-dimensional in appearance. Usually triangular, _____ arise when an object's surface is modeled, vertices are selected, and the object is rendered in a wire frame model. This is quicker to display than a shaded model; thus the _____ are a stage in computer animation.
    a. Heptadecagon
    b. Triskaidecagon
    c. Visibility polygon
    d. Polygons

19. The mathematical concept of a _____ expresses the intuitive idea of deterministic dependence between two quantities, one of which is viewed as primary and the other as secondary. A _____ then is a way to associate a unique output for each input of a specified type, for example, a real number or an element of a given set.
    a. Going up
    b. Grill
    c. Coherent
    d. Function

20. In mathematics, an average, or _____ of a data set refers to a measure of the 'middle' or 'expected' value of the data set. There are many different descriptive statistics that can be chosen as a measurement of the _____ of the data items.

An average is a single value that is meant to typify a list of values.

a. Mean reciprocal rank
b. Trimean
c. Central tendency
d. Quartile

21. In statistics, _____ has two related meanings:

- the arithmetic _____.
- the expected value of a random variable, which is also called the population _____.

It is sometimes stated that the '_____' _____s average. This is incorrect if '_____' is taken in the specific sense of 'arithmetic _____' as there are different types of averages: the _____, median, and mode. For instance, average house prices almost always use the median value for the average.

For a real-valued random variable X, the _____ is the expectation of X.

a. Statistical population
b. Proportional hazards model
c. Probability
d. Mean

22. In mathematics the concept of a _____ generalizes notions such as 'length', 'area', and 'volume'. Informally, given some base set, a '_____' is any consistent assignment of 'sizes' to the subsets of the base set. Depending on the application, the 'size' of a subset may be interpreted as its physical size, the amount of something that lies within the subset, or the probability that some random process will yield a result within the subset.

a. Cusp
b. Lattice
c. Congruent
d. Measure

23. _____ is the addition of a set of numbers; the result is their sum or total. An interim or present total of a _____ process is termed the running total. The 'numbers' to be summed may be natural numbers, complex numbers, matrices, or still more complicated objects.

a. 120-cell
b. 1-center problem
c. Summation
d. 2-3 heap

24. In mathematics, an _____, or central tendency of a data set refers to a measure of the 'middle' or 'expected' value of the data set. There are many different descriptive statistics that can be chosen as a measurement of the central tendency of the data items.

An _____ is a single value that is meant to typify a list of values.

   a. A chemical equation
   b. A posteriori
   c. A Mathematical Theory of Communication
   d. Average

25. In geometry, a _____ of a triangle is a line segment joining a vertex to the midpoint of the opposing side. Every triangle has exactly three _____s; one running from each vertex to the opposite side.

The three _____s are concurrent at a point known as the triangle's centroid, or center of mass of the triangle.

   a. Correlation
   b. Statistical significance
   c. Percentile rank
   d. Median

26. In statistics, the _____ is the value that occurs the most frequently in a data set or a probability distribution. In some fields, notably education, sample data are often called scores, and the sample _____ is known as the modal score.

Like the statistical mean and the median, the _____ is a way of capturing important information about a random variable or a population in a single quantity.

   a. Deltoid
   b. Mode
   c. Field
   d. Function

27. In optics, _____ is the phenomenon in which the phase velocity of a wave depends on its frequency. Media having such a property are termed dispersive media.

The most familiar example of _____ is probably a rainbow, in which _____ causes the spatial separation of a white light into components of different wavelengths.

a. Dispersion
b. Depth
c. Boussinesq approximation
d. Crib

28. In mathematics and statistics, _____ is a measure of difference for interval and ratio variables between the observed value and the mean. The sign of _____, either positive or negative, indicates whether the observation is larger than or smaller than the mean. The magnitude of the value reports how different an observation is from the mean.
    a. Deviation
    b. Conchoid
    c. Functional
    d. Filter

29. In probability and statistics, the _____ is a measure of the dispersion of a collection of numbers. It can apply to a probability distribution, a random variable, a population or a data set. The _____ is usually denoted with the letter σ.
    a. Statistical population
    b. Standard deviation
    c. Null hypothesis
    d. Failure rate

30. In probability theory and statistics, the _____ of a random variable, probability distribution averaging the squared distance of its possible values from the expected value. Whereas the mean is a way to describe the location of a distribution, the _____ is a way to capture its scale or degree of being spread out. The unit of _____ is the square of the unit of the original variable.
    a. Kendall tau rank correlation coefficient
    b. Nonlinear regression
    c. Probability distribution
    d. Variance

31. In elementary algebra, a _____ is a polynomial with two terms: the sum of two monomials. It is the simplest kind of polynomial except for a monomial.

The _____ $a^2 - b^2$ can be factored as the product of two other _____s:

$a^2 - b^2$ .

The product of a pair of linear _____s a x + b and c x + d is:

2 +x + bd.

A _____ raised to the n<sup>th</sup> power, represented as

n

can be expanded by means of the _____ theorem or, equivalently, using Pascal's triangle.

a. Real structure
b. Rational root theorem
c. Binomial
d. Cylindrical algebraic decomposition

32. In probability theory and statistics, the _____ is the discrete probability distribution of the number of successes in a sequence of n independent yes/no experiments, each of which yields success with probability p. Such a success/failure experiment is also called a Bernoulli experiment or Bernoulli trial. In fact, when n = 1, the _____ is a Bernoulli distribution.

a. Median
b. Biostatistics
c. Coefficient of variation
d. Binomial distribution

33. The _____ is a theorem in probability that describes the long-term stability of the mean of a random variable. Given a random variable with a finite expected value, if its values are repeatedly sampled, as the number of these observations increases, their mean will tend to approach and stay close to the expected value.

The LLN can easily be illustrated using the rolls of a die.

a. Point process
b. Graphical model
c. Law of large numbers
d. Random field

34. In statistics, a _____ is a subset of a population. Typically, the population is very large, making a census or a complete enumeration of all the values in the population impractical or impossible. The _____ represents a subset of manageable size.

a. Dispersion
b. Boussinesq approximation
c. Duality
d. Sample


35. In mathematics and physics, there are a _____ number of topics named in honor of Leonhard Euler . As well, many of these topics include their own unique function, equation, formula, identity, number, or other mathematical entity. Unfortunately however, many of these entities have been given simple names like Euler's function, Euler's equation, and Euler's formula, which are further confused by variations of the 'Euler'-prefix Overall though, Euler's work touched upon so many fields that he is often the earliest written reference on a given matter.
   a. Large
   b. List of integrals of logarithmic functions
   c. List of mathematical knots and links
   d. List of trigonometry topics


36. _____ In statistics, a result is called statistically significant if it is unlikely to have occurred by chance. "A statistically significant difference" simply means there is statistical evidence that there is a difference; it does not mean the difference is necessarily large, important, or significant in the common meaning of the word.
   a. Variance
   b. Survival analysis
   c. Confounding
   d. Statistical significance


37. Introduction

In the theory of probability and statistics, a _____ is an experiment whose outcome is random and can be either of two possible outcomes, 'success' and 'failure'.

In practice it refers to a single experiment which can have one of two possible outcomes. These events can be phrased into 'yes or no' questions:

- Did the coin land heads?
- Was the newborn child a girl?
- Were a person's eyes green?
- Did a mosquito die after the area was sprayed with insecticide?
- Did a potential customer decide to buy a product?
- Did a citizen vote for a specific candidate?
- Did an employee vote pro-union?

Therefore success and failure are labels for outcomes, and should not be construed literally. Examples of _____s include

- Flipping a coin. In this context, obverse conventionally denotes success and reverse denotes failure. A fair coin has the probability of success 0.5 by definition.
- Rolling a die, where a six is 'success' and everything else a 'failure'.
- In conducting a political opinion poll, choosing a voter at random to ascertain whether that voter will vote 'yes' in an upcoming referendum.

Mathematically, a _____ can be described by a sample space $\Omega$ consisting of two values, s for 'success' and f for 'failure'. Therefore the sample space is $\Omega = \{s, f\}$.

 a. Point process
 b. Marginal distribution
 c. Law of total cumulance
 d. Bernoulli trial

38. In scientific inquiry, an _____ is a method of investigating particular types of research questions or solving particular types of problems. The _____ is a cornerstone in the empirical approach to acquiring deeper knowledge about the world and is used in both natural sciences as well as in social sciences. An _____ is defined, in science, as a method of investigating less known fields, solving practical problems and proving theoretical assumptions.
 a. A chemical equation
 b. A posteriori
 c. A Mathematical Theory of Communication
 d. Experiment

39. In game theory, an _____ is a set of moves or strategies taken by the players, or their payoffs resulting from the actions or strategies taken by all players. The two are complementary in that given knowledge of the set of strategies of all players, the final state of the game is known, as are any relevant payoffs. In a game where chance or a random event is involved, the _____ is not known from only the set of strategies, but is only realized when the random even are realized.
 a. Equaliser
 b. Autonomous system
 c. Outcome
 d. Algebraic

40. In mathematics and in the sciences, a _____ (plural: _____e, formulæ or _____s) is a concise way of expressing information symbolically (as in a mathematical or chemical _____), or a general relationship between quantities. One of many famous _____e is Albert Einstein's E = mc$^2$ (see special relativity

## Chapter 11. Data Description and Probability Distributions 121

In mathematics, a _____ is a key to solve an equation with variables. For example, the problem of determining the volume of a sphere is one that requires a significant amount of integral calculus to solve.

a. 120-cell
b. 2-3 heap
c. 1-center problem
d. Formula

41. A _____ is a software program that facilitates symbolic mathematics. The core functionality of a CAS is manipulation of mathematical expressions in symbolic form.

The symbolic manipulations supported typically include

- simplification to the smallest possible expression or some standard form, including automatic simplification with assumptions and simplification with constraints
- substitution of symbolic, functors or numeric values for expressions
- change of form of expressions: expanding products and powers, partial and full factorization, rewriting as partial fractions, constraint satisfaction, rewriting trigonometric functions as exponentials, etc.
- partial and total differentiation
- symbolic constrained and unconstrained global optimization
- solution of linear and some non-linear equations over various domains
- solution of some differential and difference equations
- taking some limits
- some indefinite and definite integration, including multidimensional integrals
- integral transforms
- arbitrary-precision numeric operations
- Series operations such as expansion, summation and products
- matrix operations including products, inverses, etc.
- display of mathematical expressions in two-dimensional mathematical form, often using typesetting systems similar to TeX
- add-ons for use in applied mathematics such as physics packages for physical computation
- plotting graphs and parametric plots of functions in two and three dimensions, and animating them
- APIs for linking it on an external program such as a database, or using in a programming language to use the _____
- drawing charts and diagrams
- string manipulation such as matching and searching
- statistical computation
- Theorem proving and verification
- graphic production and editing such as CGI and signal processing as image processing
- sound synthesis

Many also include a programming language, allowing users to implement their own algorithms.

Some _____s focus on a specific area of application; these are typically developed in academia and are free.

a. 2-3 heap
b. 1-center problem
c. 120-cell
d. Computer algebra system

42. _____ is usually defined as the activity of using and developing computer technology, computer hardware and software. It is the computer-specific part of information technology. Computer science (or _____ science) is the study and the science of the theoretical foundations of information and computation and their implementation and application in computer systems.
    a. Deterministic finite state machine
    b. Parallel Random Access Machine
    c. Probabilistic Turing Machine
    d. Computing

43. In mathematics, specifically in combinatorial commutative algebra, a convex lattice polytope P is called _____ if it has the following property: given any positive integer n, every lattice point of the dilation nP, obtained from P by scaling its vertices by the factor n and taking the convex hull of the resulting points, can be written as the sum of exactly n lattice points in P. This property plays an important role in the theory of toric varieties, where it corresponds to projective normality of the toric variety determined by P.

The simplex in $R^k$ with the vertices at the origin and along the unit coordinate vectors is _____.

   a. Demihypercubes
   b. Normal
   c. Polytetrahedron
   d. Hypercube

44. The _____ is an important family of continuous probability distributions, applicable in many fields. Each member of the family may be defined by two parameters, location and scale: the mean and variance respectively. The standard _____ is the _____ with a mean of zero and a variance of one.
   a. Coefficient of variation
   b. Percentile rank
   c. Normal distribution
   d. Null hypothesis

## Chapter 11. Data Description and Probability Distributions

45. In probability theory, a probability distribution is called _____ if its cumulative distribution function is _____. That is equivalent to saying that for random variables X with the distribution in question, Pr[X = a] = 0 for all real numbers a. If the distribution of X is _____ then X is called a _____ random variable.
    a. Continuous
    b. Concatenated codes
    c. Continuous phase modulation
    d. Conull set

46. In probability theory, a probability distribution is called discrete if it is characterized by a probability mass function. Thus, the distribution of a random variable X is discrete, and X is then called a _____, if

$$\sum_u \Pr(X = u) = 1$$

as u runs through the set of all possible values of X.

If a random variable is discrete, then the set of all values that it can assume with non-zero probability is finite or countably infinite, because the sum of uncountably many positive real numbers always diverges to infinity.

   a. Discrete random variable
   b. First-hitting-time models
   c. Regression toward the mean
   d. Statistics

47. In mathematics, _____ are used in the study of chance and probability. They were developed to assist in the analysis of games of chance, stochastic events, and the results of scientific experiments by capturing only the mathematical properties necessary to answer probabilistic questions. Further formalizations have firmly grounded the entity in the theoretical domains of mathematics by making use of measure theory.
    a. Median polish
    b. Statistics
    c. Statistical dispersion
    d. Random variables

48. _____ is a quantity expressing the two-dimensional size of a defined part of a surface, typically a region bounded by a closed curve. The term surface _____ refers to the total _____ of the exposed surface of a 3-dimensional solid, such as the sum of the _____s of the exposed sides of a polyhedron. _____ is an important invariant in the differential geometry of surfaces.

a. A Mathematical Theory of Communication
b. A posteriori
c. Area
d. A chemical equation

49. In mathematics, hyperbolic n-space, denoted $H^n$, is the maximally symmetric, simply connected, n-dimensional Riemannian manifold with constant sectional curvature −1. _____ is the principal example of a space exhibiting hyperbolic geometry. It can be thought of as the negative-curvature analogue of the n-sphere.

   a. Margulis lemma
   b. Hyperbolic geometry
   c. Horocycle
   d. Hyperbolic space

50. An _____ is a curved shape, figure, or feature. A secant _____ of sharpness E = 120 / 100 = 1.2

In ballistics or aerodynamics, an _____ is a pointed, curved surface mainly used to form the approximately streamlined nose of a bullet, shell, missile or aircraft.

The traditional or secant _____ is a surface of revolution of the same curve that forms a Gothic arch; that is, a circular arc, of greater radius than the diameter of the cylindrical section, is drawn from the edge of the shank until it intercepts the axis.

   a. Ogive
   b. Oval
   c. Isochrone
   d. Epispiral

# ANSWER KEY

### Chapter 1
| | | | | | | | | | |
|---|---|---|---|---|---|---|---|---|---|
| 1. c | 2. c | 3. c | 4. a | 5. c | 6. b | 7. a | 8. d | 9. a | 10. d |
| 11. a | 12. d | 13. b | 14. c | 15. a | 16. b | 17. a | 18. d | 19. b | 20. b |
| 21. b | 22. a | 23. d | 24. d | 25. b | 26. b | 27. a | 28. a | 29. a | 30. d |
| 31. b | 32. d | 33. d | 34. d | 35. d | 36. d | 37. d | 38. d | 39. a | 40. d |
| 41. a | 42. c | 43. b | 44. c | 45. c | 46. c | 47. a | 48. d | 49. b | 50. a |
| 51. b | 52. b | 53. d | 54. d | | | | | | |

### Chapter 2
| | | | | | | | | | |
|---|---|---|---|---|---|---|---|---|---|
| 1. c | 2. d | 3. c | 4. c | 5. c | 6. d | 7. d | 8. c | 9. d | 10. b |
| 11. d | 12. d | 13. d | 14. d | 15. d | 16. d | 17. d | 18. d | 19. a | 20. c |
| 21. b | 22. d | 23. d | 24. b | 25. d | 26. c | 27. a | 28. d | 29. b | 30. a |
| 31. d | 32. c | 33. a | 34. d | 35. d | 36. d | 37. b | 38. a | 39. a | 40. d |
| 41. a | 42. a | 43. d | 44. d | 45. a | 46. c | 47. b | 48. b | 49. a | 50. c |
| 51. a | 52. d | 53. d | 54. c | 55. c | 56. d | | | | |

### Chapter 3
| | | | | | | | | | |
|---|---|---|---|---|---|---|---|---|---|
| 1. c | 2. a | 3. c | 4. b | 5. d | 6. d | 7. a | 8. c | 9. c | 10. d |
| 11. d | 12. a | 13. b | 14. b | 15. c | 16. d | 17. d | 18. d | 19. b | 20. a |
| 21. d | 22. a | | | | | | | | |

### Chapter 4
| | | | | | | | | | |
|---|---|---|---|---|---|---|---|---|---|
| 1. a | 2. d | 3. d | 4. d | 5. c | 6. d | 7. d | 8. d | 9. c | 10. c |
| 11. b | 12. d | 13. a | 14. a | 15. d | 16. b | 17. b | 18. d | 19. d | 20. b |
| 21. b | 22. b | 23. b | 24. d | 25. d | 26. b | 27. d | 28. c | 29. d | |

### Chapter 5
| | | | | | | | | | |
|---|---|---|---|---|---|---|---|---|---|
| 1. d | 2. c | 3. d | 4. d | 5. c | 6. a | 7. d | 8. b | 9. c | 10. d |
| 11. d | 12. d | 13. a | 14. b | 15. b | 16. a | 17. a | | | |

### Chapter 6
| | | | | | | | | | |
|---|---|---|---|---|---|---|---|---|---|
| 1. b | 2. c | 3. b | 4. c | 5. a | 6. d | 7. c | 8. b | 9. c | 10. c |
| 11. d | 12. a | 13. d | 14. b | 15. c | 16. d | 17. d | 18. d | 19. d | 20. d |
| 21. d | 22. d | 23. d | 24. d | 25. d | | | | | |

### Chapter 7
| | | | | | | | | | |
|---|---|---|---|---|---|---|---|---|---|
| 1. d | 2. d | 3. c | 4. a | 5. d | 6. d | 7. c | 8. a | 9. d | 10. b |
| 11. c | 12. a | 13. d | 14. c | 15. a | 16. d | 17. d | 18. c | 19. b | 20. d |
| 21. d | 22. d | 23. b | 24. b | 25. a | 26. c | 27. c | 28. b | 29. c | 30. a |
| 31. d | 32. d | | | | | | | | |

### Chapter 8
| | | | | | | | | | |
|---|---|---|---|---|---|---|---|---|---|
| 1. d | 2. d | 3. c | 4. d | 5. a | 6. b | 7. d | 8. b | 9. a | 10. d |
| 11. c | 12. d | 13. b | 14. d | 15. d | 16. b | 17. c | 18. d | 19. d | 20. d |
| 21. a | 22. d | 23. a | 24. b | 25. d | 26. d | 27. d | 28. b | 29. a | 30. c |
| 31. d | 32. d | 33. d | 34. d | 35. b | 36. d | 37. b | 38. d | 39. d | |

**Chapter 9**

| | | | | | | | | | |
|---|---|---|---|---|---|---|---|---|---|
| 1. c | 2. d | 3. d | 4. a | 5. b | 6. a | 7. d | 8. b | 9. d | 10. b |
| 11. d | 12. c | 13. d | 14. b | 15. d | 16. d | 17. d | 18. c | 19. d | 20. d |

**Chapter 10**

| | | | | | | | | | |
|---|---|---|---|---|---|---|---|---|---|
| 1. d | 2. d | 3. a | 4. d | 5. b | 6. d | 7. d | 8. b | 9. d | 10. c |
| 11. a | 12. b | 13. d | 14. d | 15. d | 16. a | 17. a | 18. d | 19. d | 20. d |

**Chapter 11**

| | | | | | | | | | |
|---|---|---|---|---|---|---|---|---|---|
| 1. c | 2. d | 3. a | 4. d | 5. d | 6. a | 7. c | 8. d | 9. c | 10. b |
| 11. a | 12. a | 13. d | 14. b | 15. d | 16. a | 17. d | 18. d | 19. d | 20. c |
| 21. d | 22. d | 23. c | 24. d | 25. d | 26. b | 27. a | 28. a | 29. b | 30. d |
| 31. c | 32. d | 33. c | 34. d | 35. a | 36. d | 37. d | 38. d | 39. c | 40. d |
| 41. d | 42. d | 43. b | 44. c | 45. a | 46. a | 47. d | 48. c | 49. d | 50. a |

www.ingramcontent.com/pod-product-compliance
Lightning Source LLC
Chambersburg PA
CBHW082047230426
43670CB00016B/2803